# THE BOY MY CHILDREN NEVER KNEW

# THE BOY
# MY CHILDREN
# NEVER KNEW

Rodger Johnston

NORTH STAR PRESS OF ST. CLOUD, INC.
St. Cloud, Minnesota

Published by
North Star Press of St. Cloud, Inc.
P.O. Box 451
St. Cloud, Minnesota 56302
northstarpress.com
nspress@cloudnet.com

# DEDICATION

*To my children, J. Christopher and Elizabeth Christine, with the aspiration that the memories encountered in my journey through life will endure to the benefit of their children and the generations that follow thereafter.*

# CONTENTS

# AUTHOR'S NOTE

This book is not fiction. However, to protect the privacy of those who may desire to remain unknown, some individual

names have been omitted, changed or even added as a character. In addition, some of the events surrounding the abduction remain a mystery fifty-six years later. The missing gaps were supplemented at the discretion of the author. Dramatization was employed so that the reader can share all the emotions and imagination that stirred in the boy as he traveled from one adventure to the next.

# ACKNOWLEDGEMENT

I would like to thank Lenora J. Johnson for all the time and energy put into writing a special book in 1976 for the centennial history of our community. It is entitled *Under Prairie Skies*. Her deep interest in local history was a helpful resource.

As a personal note, Mrs. J., her bestowed nickname by students, was a dedicated teacher who inspired students to go above and beyond their own expectations. With a down-to-earth personality and a genuine sincerity, she exerted a tremendous influence on those of us who embraced her enthusiasm and aspirations to succeed.

Lenora J. Johnson is shown with Gov. Harold LeVander of Minnesota. Receiving an award for winning the Minnesota Legion Oratorical contest is my cousin Jody Hovland. Jody would be the only young woman in all fifty states to advance to the high school national competition in 1968. She would finish second in the nation, a wonderful tribute to herself and "Mrs. J."

# PREFACE

THIS BOOK IS A JOURNEY through a world lost in time. From the war years of the forties into the dawn of a new era of the early fifties, each chapter shares the adventures, experiences, and memories of a boy whose wealth is not measured in dollars, but in life itself.

He is a boy equipped with an unlimited imagination and an endless source of energy committed to pursuing childhood in whatever time available. This combination of endless energy and unrestrained imagination becomes the moving force to catapult him into a maze of life provoking experiences; some of which are rather bizarre, while others border on death-defying recklessness.

Religion invokes a serene conviction that life is a divine miracle. But as with any miracle, no one can be certain why some survive beyond the norm while others perish before their time. Perhaps it is nothing more than sheer luck. Then again, maybe some things are predetermined. As for the boy, his life evolves precariously one day at a time in a world he does not visualize as good or evil, moral or immoral, safe or dangerous. It is a world just there for the taking, a challenging environment full of abundant opportunities to explore, learn and enjoy in whatever capacity available. For him, the real tragedy is not in dying, but in never living.

In the end, the boy and the writer are inevitably merged in ways never thought possible. Collectively they discover there is no escape from the past as there can be no escape from the truth. But as truth can set one free, the chapters not only liberate the memoirs of the writer from within, but he is also freed to consciously evolve within his own cycle of life from beginning to end.

# INTRODUCTION

*We shall journey only once through life,*
*Where time is the true source of wealth.*
*Therefore, do not hesitate to be all you can be,*
*For you will never share this life again.*

RJJ

EACH OF US is destined to take many different journeys in life. But none will be more compelling or more fulfilling than the journey to deliver an insight into the genesis of our own existence as we explore our early childhood. And although the reverse passage from adult to childhood may seem impossible, nevertheless, time travel is still accessible by probing the early memory hidden deep within each of us. It is a journey where time becomes the lens through which we capture a view of how the past plays an integral part in who we have become.

This book is a passageway into a time long forgotten. It unearths a place where memories are shrouded in darkness and the connection between past and present seems lost. However, like an old journal abandoned and neglected for fifty years in a far away attic, the memories remain etched deep within. Covered in layers of forgotten dust, they wait patiently to be uncovered.

Like every child born fortunate to inherit the wealth of time, we follow a boy marching to his own beat to experience life in any way possible. And when he eventually abandons his "never, never land" of adolescence and journeys to manhood, he unknowingly carries the boy's past deep within his unconscious being.

Raised in a heritage rich in courage and creativity, but lean in education and material possessions, his creative imagination and determination is focused beyond the horizon. Even the imaginary fence surrounding a humble "Shanty Town" origin does not become an impediment.

Never looking back, he learns to accept nothing less than the best he can be. Every defeat spurs an open challenge to succeed. Obstacles are readily accepted as an invitation evoking a creative solution. And while book learning provides knowledge to open doors, his inventive imagination opens worlds. As for failure, it remains a luxury only the poor at heart have time to contemplate.

In the end, deeds will speak louder than words of improbability. And in the autumn of my life, I would come to realize that the man and the father were not much different from "The Boy My Children Never Knew."

# THE BOY MY CHILDREN NEVER KNEW

Rodger, holding a birthday cake in the backyard thirty days prior to being kidnapped.

# CHAPTER ONE

# KIDNAPPED

IT WAS 10:15 A.M. Just a month earlier, the family celebrat-ed my sixth birthday. As the morning sun illuminated the backyard, three neighborhood children busily played with their toys in the flower bed. Nearby, a narrow grass alley split the yard in half. There was nothing unusual about that summer day except for one exciting difference. The circus had come to town.

The arrival of the circus each summer became a high-light in the life of every child. In fact, the entire community would transcend itself into an atmosphere of festivity. Eagerly they awaited the colored carriages bringing both the spectacu-lar and the unexpected.

As the giant locomotive drew near, the engineer an-nounced the arrival of the circus by blasting his steam whistle in long, ear-shattering intervals. With the other hand, he forced the massive iron horse to spout clouds of steam high into the air. In response, the crowds of townsfolk shouted and waved to show their approval. Utmost in their mind was to capture a glimpse of the many curiosities and abnormalities hidden within the dark, secret confinement of the decorated wooden boxcars.

The real show did not begin until the circus unloaded its cargo on a sidetrack at the far end of Main Street. From there, animals and performers organized into columns and paraded down the paved thoroughfare. The once peaceful streets were soon filled with a joyful, yet fearful, reverence for the new visitors. Marching to music, the circus people would entice and entertain the multitudes of cheering onlookers. The pandemonium never ceased until the parade reached the wired enclosure of the county fairgrounds.

There in the normally quiet prairie field, the circus town unfolded in the blink of an eye. Onlookers were treated to the awesome sound and spectacular sights of the circus coming together piece by piece.

Dad and I watching the circus unload on the sidetrack one day prior to the kidnapping.

For me, the interaction of man and beast working side by side as though they were longtime partners was the ultimate breath-taking experience. And, of all the four-footed creatures, none were more exciting than the ivory-tusked giants of Africa. In size and strength, these ancient cousins of ice-age mammoths proved to be the true King of Beasts. When hitched to leather harnesses, one could actually feel the ground vibrate as feet the size of watermelons stomped the earth. Their powerful trunks poised like mechanical cranes as they lifted enormous poles into place beneath the huge canvas.

The thrilling finale came when elephant and man stood shoulder to shoulder to raise the big top. With backs curved and heads lowered, each gray mountain of muscle would tug and pull until every inch of its body began to quiver. Then from somewhere deep within their belly came a rumbling as the backbreaking weight of the entire canvas slowly lifted into the sky to become a gigantic balloon. If a person had the courage to stand close enough, they could actually absorb the sensation of the elephants' energy raining from their pores.

Just as every city has a main street, the circus had its own main street. Stretching for more than a block, visitors were treated to an endless variety of creepy and mind-boggling sideshows. Each brightly colored tapestry offered a tantalizing sneak preview of the freakish performers hidden within: The Snakeman, The Fat Lady, The Sword Swallower, The Two-Headed Pigmy, or The Man Who Slept on a Bed of Nails. Hawkers challenged onlookers to venture behind the canvas doorway. They guaranteed a spine-tingling aberration that would shock and amaze.

In the midst of all this excitement, the passageway to the Big Top was also home to the unforgettable, goofy clowns performing comical interactions with any spectator foolish enough to oblige. The cautious ones always fared best. They scurried for cover to avoid the mischievous behavior while others became the focus of tear-provoking laughter that clouded the air thicker than a fog.

Adding to this euphoria were the irresistible sights and smells of large balls of pink cotton candy, warm caramel apples, fresh buttered popcorn, and chocolate-covered ice cream sandwiches. Few could resist the tantalizing aroma of hotdogs smothered in onions simmering over a hot grill. Add a draft of homemade root beer and all was good. The circus food, the thrills, and heart-throbbing encounters made the circus the best place to be in the entire world.

However, within this magical fantasy lived a vicious predator. When he emerged, he set into motion a course of events that would catastrophically collide with my small world. And whatever the final outcome, it was destined to alter life seriously or end it altogether. The day the man from the circus trespassed into my innocent world became my "Day That Would Live in Infamy."

It was still 10:15 a.m. Sunlight dappled the yard where three young boys were busily playing and talking about the circus. Living only two blocks from the fairgrounds, we could hear the elephants trumpeting and the clash of iron stakes being driven into the ground.

Suddenly and unexpectedly, a stranger appeared from out of nowhere. Undoubtedly, he had skulked down the grassy alley from the fairgrounds. He halted when he noticed us. As the tall, burly man stared down at the three boys, we could not help but notice a puffy face with deep lines that created a trail of shadows from chin to forehead. The texture of both checks was also defined by a series of cracks crisscrossing from a wide mouth to a set of thick, protruding eyebrows.

When he extended a hand to offer us a free ticket to the circus, the column of matted, dark hair blanketing his arm was a perfect match to the unruly, black hair on his head. I had observed other men just like him at the carnival. Mom referred to these men as "Carnies."

No one looked directly at the stranger. We continued to play in the dirt, pretending the man did not exist. The intruder cleared his throat to get our attention. He announced that he had been specially selected by the circus to walk through the community to offer free tickets to all the performances. The phrase "free tickets" immediately struck a friendly chord.

The very thought of free tickets was very tempting. It held more enticement than the free matinee offered at the Orpheum Theater during Christmas holidays. Soon my mind became absorbed with the notion of a free pass to a world of adventures. But, the man's offer had one small catch. Whoever decided to accept his offer would have to accompany him to the other parts of the neighborhood to distribute the rest of the free passes. He was quick to add that the journey would not take long, so whoever decided to come would return long before anyone noticed.

Immediately, my two playmates glanced at each other with troubled looks. They shook their heads to signal that they were not interested. Their mother had given strict orders not to leave our yard for any reason. And, if those orders were disobeyed, they would not be allowed to attend the circus at all. For them, free tickets would be of no benefit.

However, my mom had not dictated such an ultimatum. She had no reason to. After all, her son was merely playing in his own backyard. Why would she have reason to suspect that he might leave, especially with a complete stranger? And if it had not been for the deep, passionate, lure of the circus, I believe Mom would have been correct in her assumption. Unfortunately, my fate came down to a combination of being in the right place at the wrong time. In addition, the bait the stranger offered could not have been more tempting.

As we departed, I remember being completely mesmerized by the prospect of receiving free tickets. With spirits high,

I soon became lost in my own thoughts. Oblivious to danger, I failed to take notice that we were moving toward the south edge of the neighborhood in the direction of the river.

However, as we approached the tall, grassy field marking the boundary between town and country, an uncomfortable feeling covered me like a cloud. I had finally realized that something was not quite right. We should have been walking in a different direction if we intended to canvass the neighborhood as the man had earlier promised.

The stranger was quick to recognize my reluctance when my legs refused to move. He mumbled some words about a change of plan as he reached down and took a firm hold on my arm. At that crucial moment when joy and fear clash unexpectedly one's thoughts begin to flood with confusion. The mind signals the body to run, but the connection has somehow been severed. It's as though one's senses were set adrift in a time vacuum.

I remember closing my eyes and thinking, "What's happening? Where are we going?"

When the stranger said, "Everything is going to be just fine," his words of assurance did not provide any comfort. His tight grip around my arm had a different message. With or without my cooperation, I would either continue or face the prospect of being dragged.

As we slogged through the field, apprehension mushroomed into a waking nightmare. I seemed to linger in a dream world where my heart yearned to dash home, but the mind still refused to coordinate the urgent message to run. My only response was to drag my foot to slow the pace. I had to try something. Who knows, maybe something good might come of it.

However, the stranger was not about to allow our pace to be slowed by a dragging foot. He had other plans. Yanking at my arm, he forced a steady pace.

What is it like to be kidnapped at age six? First came a dark, lonely feeling that enveloped all my senses. Then my mind introduced me to terror beyond my imagination. Once captured in the grasp of that fear, my mind began to relay a series of intermittent messages that something awful was about to happen. But I wasn't certain what this evil was or when it would strike. Yet, I knew it was hovering ever so close. Clutched securely in the grasp of sudden, unexpected harm, one's only companions are despair and futility. And as I reached that critical point of no return, life began to crumble into a blur with an uncertain outcome.

Fortunately, most children will never experience abduction. But for those of us who do and survive, trust me, we never forget. It is said that God is happiest when his children are at play. If so, God must be at his saddest when his children are abducted by evil.

As the carnie continued to drag my limp body through the tall grass, I kept looking over my shoulder. I was hoping to see Mom or Dad in pursuit. I refused to relinquish the hope that they would come to my rescue. Faith in my parents was strong. Nothing could take that away. They had always been by my side whenever I had needed them. Now that need was greater than it had ever been. It was almost as great as my hope. But, unbeknown to me, the clock had begun to tick as the race for life or death was under way.

Growing to adulthood, I often wondered if other abducted children shared a similar feeling. For me, Mom and Dad had become synonymous with hope. And although there were forces beyond my control trying to take everything away, one thing could not be taken away. It was the hope Mom or Dad would be reaching out for me, especially Mom; her presence seemed constantly to hover before my eyes.

Contrary to my own thoughts of doom and gloom, beyond the grassy field all hope had not yet been lost.

Following my departure with the stranger, my playmates had immediately returned home. When their mother inquired as to why they had come home early, they explained what happened. Most important, they reported that the stranger I followed was a man from the carnival.

Perhaps, if they had not mentioned the "carnival man," everything might have turned out differently. But those two words automatically triggered an immediate alarm. It was as though a fire siren had been blown within the confines of this mother's brain.

Realizing the urgency of the situation, she immediately placed a phone call to Mom who was answering a knock at the door. It was a young girl who reported that she had seenRodger walking with a strange man. Troubled and confused, Mom rushed to answer the phone. The voice on the other end confirmed every mother's worst nightmare. Her son had been taken away by a "carnie." On the verge of hysteria, she fumbled with the phone waiting for the operator to answer. Fortunately, the phone operator on duty was Dad's sister. We called this aunt "Dot" because Dorothea was too hard to pronounce. She was an exceptionally experienced operator with a quick mind. In fact, her father, who was my grandfather, William Johnston, had worked for the same

"Dot" was my favorite aunt, who fiercely protected the family.

8

local telephone company. Sadly, he had drowned a few years earlier in the flooded waters of the Red River.

As a proficient telephone operator, my aunt knew everyone as well as everything there was to know about everybody in the community. In the late 1940s, direct dialing service did not yet exist. To place a telephone call, the procedure required physical intervention by a switchboard operator. When a caller lifted the receiver, the operator responded by saying, "Number please." Once the operator secured the telephone number to be called, they plugged in an appropriate connection into the big switchboard causing the phone of the other party to ring. Then every "good" operator would monitor the call until the other party answered and sometimes a little bit longer. In short, no telephone conversation was ever private.

Dot immediately recognized Mom's voice despite the quavering sounds she managed to squeeze out of her throat. Eventually, the message came across explaining that a carnival man had abducted me from the backyard. Now within the same family, two entirely different responses emerged. Mom broke down and began crying uncontrollably. Her voice echoed a distinct tone of desperation. On the other hand, my aunt, accustomed to emergencies as a phone operator, immediately clicked into a heightened readiness. She was prepared to do battle.

Convincing Mom to get off the line, she suggested it would be very helpful if Mom checked with the neighbors for any additional information. Auntie Dot assured Mom that all the necessary calls would be made to alert the authorities. With nimble fingers, she had already inserted a line to the constable's home. How did she know where to call at that precise moment? Well, it just so happened the constable had placed a call to his wife a few minutes earlier telling her he would be coming for morning coffee. By coincidence, my aunt just happened to overhear that conversation.

When the constable lifted the receiver this time, auntie rattled off a complete summary of the abduction. Before their conversation ended, the constable knew that a man from the carnival had abducted her nephew who was only six years old. The approximate time of abduction was forty minutes prior to her call. The direction the carnie and I were last known to be traveling was toward the south edge of town. And, we were on foot.

Minutes were crucial. A constable of the late forties did not have the advantage of modern-day technology or even full-time deputies. In addition, he did not have the benefit of statistical data that would have disclosed to him that harm to a young child abducted by a non-family adult will occur within the first twenty-four hours. Most died within forty-eight hours.

What he did have was a keen instinct combined with street-smart experience that had been fine-tuned over time. He was a self-made man backed by the full weight of the law and the community. Intuitively, he already knew the urgency of the situation, that his time for achieving a good outcome would be measured in minutes, not hours.

As for me, time had no more meaning. I just wanted to shrivel up and disappear. What remained was a small part of me still clinging to the hope of parental rescue. It was the only thing that kept me going.

Trekking under the shadow of a giant of a man and being forced to walk faster than I wanted wore me out. The sun washed waves of heat across the field. When we reached a mid-point in the field, the stranger unexpectedly came to a halt. He said he had to go to the bathroom.

As the carnie stood tall against the sky, I noticed his weather-beaten face appeared flushed from the heat. His short-sleeved shirt was soaked from the sweat seeping uncontrollably from his hairy arms. When finished, he sat on the ground and faced the sun with his legs crossed. He then instructed me to sit directly in front of him.

Too terrified not to obey, I sat down. Mesmerized before this monster of a man, I had no way of knowing what he might do next. And even if I might have been able to do something, his piercing eyes staring from beneath a massive set of dark eyebrows held me immobile.

Worse yet, I was surrounded by a column of air that was choked with the rancid stench from his sweaty body. My heart pounded as I found myself staring adversity directly in the eye. I could not begin to imagine what this man was thinking, but deep inside, I felt things were about to go from bad to worse. And they did.

Slipping his hand into the zipper of his pants he began to jerk his hand up and down. He insisted I carefully observe his every movement. Desperate to escape, I wanted to turn away, but I was too scared of the consequences if I failed to obey.

Eventually, the motion of his hand quickened. Then he paused for a moment, took a deep breath and began again. But this time he insisted I join in. When I hesitated, he grabbed the back of my wrist with the grip of an iron wrench. Firmly within his control, he forced me into participating. For the first time since the abduction, my mind was seduced by the images of a terrible ending. I felt I had been entombed in a small bottle with no chance of escape.

Meanwhile, the constable had taken his own steps to formulate a plan that had an image of a different ending. Like every good law enforcement officer, he knew every inch of his territory. Mentally, he visualized the river's tributary flowing along the eastern edge of the large, grass field. He also pictured the dirt road running to the west of the field. Together the two natural boundaries created a funnel. Anyone walking would be inclined to follow this landscape to the main river.

Faster and more creative than a computer, the constable was ready to implement his plan of action.

No one in our community ever doubted that the constable was anything less then very competent. A tough veteran of more than his share of skirmishes, he was unconditionally accepted as the designated guardian of the community. He had acquired the expertise for his trade from example and by trial and error. It had made him smart beyond book learning.

And like other constables of the time, he took his commitment to protecting the lives of every citizen very seriously. This code of honor by which he lived was sacred and utmost in his mind. It was not a pretentious code of mere words. It was a deep, spiritual commitment he would never abandon.

When America was forced to fight in World War II to preserve our way of life, law enforcement officers were delegated the "absolute" responsibility to protect their own communities. It was unconditional. They would be entrusted to do whatever they deemed necessary "to serve" and "to protect."

In small communities like our own, that dedicated protectorate resided in the constable. His authority became unprecedented and never challenged. And unlike his modern-day counterparts, he had inherited a wide degree of latitude in the unwritten rules of the law. It was an undefined code of rules that could encompass the principle that the end sometimes justified the means.

As for my abductor, he had stepped outside any definition of the law.

Confused and frightened, my body began to tremble. And as the horror of the unknown continued, I became completely numb sitting in the hot sun. Then, without any warning, the stranger lurched forward and began to groan involuntarily. When he stopped, my wet, sticky hand was finally permitted to withdraw. As he stood up, he stretched his arms upward into the sky and took a deep sigh.

Whatever strange event had occurred, it was far beyond the understanding of a six-year old. As I peered upward from ground level, my captor's sweat-drenched face had taken on a reddish appearance. The bright sun also revealed a tattoo below his belt line. I had no way of knowing that my fate had reached a critical juncture. It was a moment in time when the price of my innocence was no longer an affordable option. For some children in my position, it was often a time when they vanished into the dream world and were never seen again.

Meanwhile, back at the station, the constable was still pursuing his own vision of my future. With a little coordination and a lot of good old-fashioned know-how, his hastily improvised plan was ready to be set into motion. As commander in chief, he proceeded to institute instructions that were precise and unwavering.

His first order to my aunt was to call his part-time deputy. She would brief him on the situation and then direct him to drive his vehicle to the small road beyond the river south of town. There he was to wait and be prepared to apprehend anyone attempting to cross the river.

His next order was to sound the fire alarm. When the fire chief answered, she was to instruct the chief to take his firemen and trucks along the state highway heading to the south beyond the first bridge. From that point, they would form a perimeter parallel to the grassy fields on the far side of the railroad tracks. If anyone spotted a man running toward the tracks, they were to do anything necessary to apprehend him.

The final order was for Dot to contact the neighbors on the south edge of town near the grassy field. She was to seek whatever assistance they could render. Back then, neighbors were acquainted by more than just a name. They were resourceful and caring. The constable knew that the meaning of family transcended the boundary lines of their own yards or their own families.

As for the constable, he planned to cover the county dirt road that extended south, parallel to the fairgrounds. If his plan worked, the man would be trapped in a box from which he could not escape. The constable was also aware that my father was a volunteer fireman. But, as Dad rushed to the station to volunteer his services he had no idea that the urgency was to save his own son.

I stiffened my resolved not to move any further, but my abductor once again clamped down on my arm and resumed his path towards the river. Apparently, he had a specific destination in mind. But I was too indifferent to care and my legs too wobbly to walk. Wherever we were destined to go, time no longer mattered. It had become painfully clear that any possibility of rescue was not coming.

For my aunt, time did matter. Like a well-trained trooper, she followed her orders explicitly. With nimble fingers, she removed every phone connection on the town's switchboard. The normal morning chit-chatting conversations suddenly came to an abrupt end. Auntie had declared martial law, and no unnecessary conversation would be connected until the emergency ended. Simultaneously, she activated the city siren. Within seconds volunteer firemen began racing to the fire hall from every corner of the community to report for duty.

Meanwhile, my captor and I had reached an area where the field ended. Here the land began to rise to a crest overlooking the river. By now, any remaining energy left in my small frame was strictly reserved for breathing. Complete exhaustion coupled with isolation and fear had replaced all other feelings.

If I ever had a slim chance to escape, it was gone. I could barely keep going. I couldn't even hear the sound of the town siren blasting the call to arms. And it apparently continued to wail long after the volunteers had reported to duty. Auntie must have wanted the entire community to go on full battle station alert.

Once the fire chief had been briefed, Auntie's attention was directed to residents on the south edge of town. Injecting line plugs into five or six connections at a time, telephones began to ring throughout the southern neighborhood. As residents answered, they were quickly informed as to the plight of Dot's young nephew. She pleaded with every neighbor to help in whatever capacity they could to save his life.

The information Dot gave over the phone was then circulated by word of mouth. So effective were her efforts that a battalion of residents soon assembled, and they were armed with metal shovels, forks, and rakes. Fortunately, one neighbor had actually observed a man and a small boy crossing the grassy field, heading in the direction of the river. With that critical intelligence, the neighborhood brigade charged into the field. They began shouting their own battle cry as someone spotted the silhouette of a large man in the distant landscape.

At that same point in time, we were about to climb down the embankment to the river. For reasons unknown, the man stopped at the edge of the cliff. He appeared extremely troubled. He turned a hundred and eighty degrees, looking in the direction from which we had traveled.

His first reaction was to crouch low to the ground as if to avoid being seen. His next motion was to move to the highest point for a better view. As he glanced nervously out over the field, he began to murmur a series of disjointed phrases followed by a bobbing of his head. Finally, he turned his attention once again towards the river.

When he stared down at me, his jaws were clenched. His fiery eyes were sending me a message of doom. Without any warning, he lifted my small frame high into the sky and flung me over the crest of the cliff. My body sailed through the air like a piece of driftwood.

Slamming into the side of the sandy embankment, I began to roll towards the rushing water. Within inches of a watery grave, I came to a sudden stop. My little arm had fortuitously snagged a crusted cone-shaped mogul.

Cattle approaching the river to drink at the river's edge often created these moguls or hummocks by walking in their same foot imprints repeatedly. Now that peculiar quirk from within the animal world was about to become an unlikely lifesaver.

With the crushing force of the fall, the remaining air escaped. The combination of an absence of breath and the shock of the impact rendered me unconscious. Just moments before, I remembered closing my eyes. Now both the nightmare and I would vanish into the same darkness.

Faced with the prospect of being caught, the abductor had attempted to cover his tracks by eliminating all evidence. I'm sure he intended that I be swept away by the river. Neighbors who reached the crest were grief stricken to see a child's seemingly lifeless body lying so near to the river's edge. My short-sleeved shirt and blue jeans were smeared with dirt and grass stains.

The pale apparition of my still body left an impression on many of them. Instead of the normal flesh color, my face was faintly gray with a dark blue shadow around my lips. The youthful gleam of innocence inherent in all children at this tender age had all but disappeared. It was replaced with an indescribably desolate mask commonly observed in funeral parlors. No one was certain if they should approach what appeared to be a dead body.

Meanwhile, the constable had observed the commotion from the dirt road. With siren blazing, his patrol car plowed through the field to the crest above the river. Before he could come to a complete stop, the squad car door flew wide open. Leaping out, he immediately yelled an order for everyone to stand back. When the constable peered over the crest and spotted my motionless body, he jumped over the embankment. He scrambled to maintain a foothold in the loose sand as he worked his way over to my motionless body. He then lowered himself to one knee to determine if my time had expired. Discovering that life had not yet taken flight, the community's protectorate lifted my small frame gently into his muscular arms. He then proudly announced, "He's alive!"

Upon hearing the good news, a jubilant cheer rose from all who had come forward to save the young boy's life.

I do not believe anyone present on that day was more relieved than the town constable. Unknown to me until fifty years later, I was more than just any little boy. I was the grandson of a very close friend, a friend who had not only been a constable of the city for many years, but had recently died a tragic death before his time.

The very notion of being a pallbearer a second time and laying his friend's grandson to rest next to his grandfather's fresh grave would have been more painful than he would have ever wanted to acknowledge. I also learned that when Grandpa's body was lowered into the ground, the brotherhood within law enforcement had made a solemn pledge. They would look after their friend's grandchildren like guardian angels.

As one of the neighbors came forward to assist the constable, the remaining rescuers triumphantly returned to their homes. The neighbor who volunteered to assist now held my unconscious body in his arms. Once in the constable's car, the engine roared as it crossed the open field. Columns of dust marked the trail. The destination was home, not a grave as many had feared.

In the days that followed, the neighbor who accompanied the constable shared his first-hand report of the news in every local coffee shop. Apparently, the constable had bestowed the abductor with the name "Son-of-a-Bitch." All things considered, the constable's rescue plan had worked flawlessly. The deputy had successfully taken "Son-of-a-Bitch" into custody by the time the constable returned to the station.

According to sources, the deputy parked his car as instructed out beyond the river. While patiently waiting, he spotted a man running on the opposite side of the river. As soon as the man waded across, he made his capture by chasing the fugitive down with his vehicle. One final revelation the neighbor shared was that "Son-of-a-Bitch" could expect to experience the wrath of a very angry constable.

After a few days allowing me calm and rest, Mom and Dad gingerly began to inquire about the ordeal. But for me, the ordeal was a nightmare I truly wanted to forget. It had been buried at the edge of the river. This was especially true concerning any recollection as to what the man had forced me to do. And as painful as the experience had been, I could take refuge in the knowledge that this dirty secret was mine alone forever.

However, Dad was persistent in his questioning after the abduction. He pressed hard for the secret knowledge I would not share. Thankfully, Mom intervened and told him, "Maybe someday he'll tell us more, but no one is going to make him talk if he doesn't want to."

Then, for some unexplained reason, the episode was never discussed in conversation again, not even by Dad. I'm certain outside the family circle rumors spreading through the grapevine suggested that there was much more to this incident than anyone might ever find out. Little did they realize, their chatty talk did have a ring of truth to it.

The drama of the abduction did not end without one final episode. Dad insisted that I accompany him to the jail to identify my abductor. He promised both Mom and me that the trip would not take long. Of course, the last thing I wanted was to come face to face with the man in my nightmare. But, in the end, nothing could prevent Dad from having his way.

The local jail was situated in the rear of a two-story brick building housing the fire trucks. The entrance to the jail was through a single door facing Main Street. As we entered the narrow passageway leading into the constable's office, Dad reached down and placed my tiny hand in the palm of his large hand. No doubt, he was attempting to provide some sort of assurance that there would be no danger.

As we entered the office, the constable rose from behind his large oak desk pushed tight up against the wall. After a brief conversation, we followed him down a narrow, dark corridor to an iron door. There he inserted a large key that had been hanging from his belt. As the iron door creaked opened, an unexpected gush of air was issued from within the cell area. The odor was reminiscent of an outhouse with the mixed aroma of puke added for good measure. The only thing missing was a Sears-Roebuck catalog.

The wide open corridor led us past a maze of iron-barred cells on one side and a series of irregular brick on the other. The ceiling was exceptionally high with small, iron-barred windows near the top. Light filtered through only a few of these dusty windows. Only a small fraction of that natural light ever reached the floor.

In addition to the stench and the dim surroundings, I remembered the air was musty and damp, like in a dirt cellar. The bare, concrete floors were cold.

Whether it was from fright or the raw, cold air, goose bumps erupted on my arms as we made our way along the dingy corridor. The room was scary in and of itself. The only bars of iron I had ever experienced were used to restrain dangerous animals like man-eating lions or bone-crushing bears.

When we finally reached the end of the corridor, we stopped. As I glared through the narrow, iron bars, I saw the shadow of a man crouched low to the concrete floor in the last cell. My first impression was of a scared animal hunkering down to protect itself from danger. With clothes tattered and bloody hair snarled, he exuded a strong nauseating smell.

As I stared at the crumbled body before me, I had mixed feelings of being glad and sad. Glad because the monster in my nightmare was no longer a threat in the condition he was in and with him in a closed cell. I was sad because his crumbled body stained with blood was a reflection of myself only a few days earlier.

The constable growled an order for the man in the cell to stand. The sound of his powerful and authoritative voice boomed through the entire jail. Slowly the man in the cell lifted his arms and made a feeble attempt to rise from the floor.

"Stand up" shouted the constable for a second time.

As the man slowly began to stand, my hands clutched tightly onto my father's pants leg. Sensing my fear, Dad peered down and asked, "Is this the man who took you away?"

At first, I didn't respond. It was difficult to look directly at the man. I wanted to avoid making eye contact, fearing the memory of those dark eyes reflecting only doom. Eventually, I peeked from behind my father's leg. Immediately I recognized the same dark, hairy arms that had taken me prisoner with an iron grip. And although the face was now blazing red with eyes sunken deeply, those unmistakable heavy pair of dark eyebrows confirmed his identity for me.

There was no doubt that the man in the cell was the same man who had taken me away. After several more glances, I nodded my head up and down to signify my guilty verdict. Unbeknown to me, the constable's eyes had been fixed on my response. When he noticed my nod, he met Dad's eyes. After a few moments of silence, the only words spoken by the constable were, "That is all we need to know."

Dad then took me by the hand and, with the constable flanking me on the other side, we retreated from the iron cages. On our way out, my eyes strayed nowhere but stared straight ahead. Finally, the metal door closed behind us with a loud clang of iron striking against iron.

Once outside the building, the fresh air and the warmth of the sun provided a comforting relief. I remember repeating silently, "It's over." "It's finally over." For me, the will to make a bad memory go away was not a cure, only a wish. And it was a wish that would last for a long time. No one could ever make me tell the dirty secret without my consent.

Over the years, no family member, including Dad, Mom, Granny, or my Aunt Dot, ever brought up the subject of the abduction again. They had also never discussed the fact that Grandfather had been a constable for many years. My brother, who was five years older, did not learn of the abduction until fifty years later when he read a rough draft of this book.

Cloaked in mystery, I was sure that each member of my family had reasons to forget or deny what had happened to me. Both Dad and my aunt were fiercely loyal to the family. They would have made good secret agents. If captured, no one would be able to get them to talk. And if they did talk, they would never reveal a secret. Only Mom would be willing to share what she knew, but only after Dad died. And like other family members, I too had never shared the personal aspect of the story until now.

Strangely enough, when I attended the all-school reunion in 2001, an elderly lady in a wheelchair stared at me and said, "I remember you. You're the little boy who was kidnapped."

For a moment I was dumb-founded. Fifty-two years had passed. Who would have assumed that the memory had remained in a non-family person? But it did. Her name was Dorothy Ruoff. Our families were both members of the First Methodist church. Her husband, Dan, had been a beloved teacher and athletic coordinator in the community for a lifetime. During my college years, he had hired me as a lifeguard and swimming instructor for the community pool. For reasons unknown, she had not remembered those things. But Dorothy had preserved the memory of that day when I was taken from my home against my will.

For me, it would take twenty years from the time of my abduction before another jail incident caused my buried memory to surface unexpectedly. When it did, I was compelled to reexamine the prospect of what may have happened to the man left behind in a dark cell so many years before.

As a recent law school graduate, my first introduction to the practice of law included an induction into the newly created Public Defender Program. Supreme Court decisions in the 1960s had begun a process that would soon revolutionize the criminal justice system. Cases such as Escobedo, Miranda, and a host of others had extended the United States Constitution in ways never before dreamed possible. They made it clear that those charged with a crime had an undeniable right to an attorney. If they were unable to afford the services of an attorney of their choosing, the court was legally bound to provide one without cost.

The public defender program had been created to make sure that the new laws would be implemented as the Supreme Court had envisioned them. And we who were the early pioneers in this new system of justice would play an indispensable role in that revolutionary change as we provided legal services to indigents accused of a felony. Traveling from courthouse to courthouse across central Minnesota and from one jail to the next, I experienced a unique view into the life of the criminal.

The unexpected personal bonus that came with the job was that it brought me into direct contact with county sheriffs. These same county sheriffs had been constables during the period when I was kidnapped. It seemed that the position of small-town constable had functioned as an informal apprenticeship to the higher office of county sheriff.

Since public defenders represented those who were financially destitute, it should come as no surprise that most of the public defender clientele were unable to raise bail. Under those circumstances, they often remained in jail. This provided a perfect opportunity to become personally acquainted with the sheriff in each county on his own turf. I use the term "turf" to include the jailhouse.

The local jails in our rural counties were also home to the sheriff and his entire family. At the time, living accommodations provided one of the fringe benefits of the job. However, there was one small additional contingency. The sheriff's wife had to either cook or make other arrangements for the meals provided to the inmates residing in the back half of their residence, the jail.

To be an attorney working the legal system in the late 1960s and early 1970s was different from the time when I was kidnapped as a little boy in the 1940s. Unlike at the time of the abduction, I was now in the right place at the right time. I would witness first hand the end of one era of law enforcement and the beginning of a new one. But what was especially important, I would get up close and personal with those who were in law enforcement for most of the twentieth century, before and after these legal changes.

Every county sheriff I had encountered seemed to lay claim to their badge longer than they could remember. Without a doubt, most were old enough to have been constables when my nightmare had unfolded. Working the jailhouse circuit, I began to probe and document the behavior of these crime fighters of the past.

What I discovered was that the administration of the law by the current sheriff as compared to when they were constables in the 1940s had not changed. And although the times were changing around them, their *modus operandi* in enforcing the law remained the same. They too had become locked in a time vacuum.

One of many incidents that would confirm my conclusion happened one Monday morning when I received a list of qualified defendants from the Clerk of Court. The first stop on my list was a defendant in the local lockup a block from my office. Most places of confinement were off limits to visitors and attorneys before breakfast. However, on this particular day, the jail entrance was bolted long after the normal breakfast period. Being acquainted with the sheriff's family, I decided to make my way to the jail through their private residence. It offered an easy second entrance into the jail.

Noticing that the door on the porch had been left open, I rapped on the screen. There was no answer. Having entered the jail by this route on previous occasions, I announced my presence and quickly proceeded through the narrow hallway leading directly into the jail. Upon opening the large, steel door, I was greeted by our sheriff. He was stretching a man six inches off the floor with one hand secured tightly around his neck.

Interestingly, my presence neither disturbed nor distracted the sheriff's work in progress. In fact, he calmly requested I help myself to the chair located by the iron door. Taken aback, I accepted. Little did I realize I had been offered a ringside seat for what was about to be the major bout of the day. However, in this contest the combatants were not evenly matched. The rules of engagement were fixed. Only the sheriff was permitted to use physical force.

By the end of round three, the man's face showed clear signs of stress. His color had become a mixture of bright red and dark blue. When the man's head dropped to his chest, he appeared physically drained. He gasped for air like a guppy out of water. Regardless of his condition, the sheriff once more wrapped his hands around the man's neck and lifted the prisoner into the air before flinging his body across the room. The man slammed into the wall and came crashing to the concrete floor near my feet.

One thing was for certain. Law School had failed to include this scenario in their curriculum. The time had come to improvise. I stood up straight and tall to establish a semblance of importance. With an authoritative voice, I demanded to know what exactly the sheriff was trying to accomplish. In response, the sheriff calmly told me that I needed to take my seat. His tone was firm. He went on to state, "This is not a confrontation, merely a routine interrogation."

Apparently, the prisoner had been withholding information concerning accomplices responsible for stealing batteries from the local implement dealer. According to the sheriff, he was merely asking the boy to furnish the other names. He was quick to point out that my client apparently failed to understand the situation. The sheriff was not making a request, but an inescapable demand.

No doubt his procedure would save a lot of investigative work and taxpayer dollars if the prisoner relinquished the names. Such a favorable outcome justified the means.

The sheriff made it perfectly clear that he would not tolerate any further interference. Especially not from an uninvited guest, attorney or no attorney, who had sneaked into "his" jail without his permission. My choices were to either return to my seat or quietly leave the same way I had come. Fascinated by how nonchalantly law enforcement operated in the privacy of their world, I chose to remain.

During our brief exchange, I could not help but notice the man lying on the floor had curled into a ball to protect himself from additional punishment. As I gazed down at the crumbled body stained in blood, the scene unexpectedly triggered a memory of another silhouette in a jail a lifetime ago.

Then, from out of nowhere, the once-buried memory from the past suddenly jumped into my consciousness. It had always been hanging around, but I had chosen to ignore it. By day's end, I had no other choice. This incident forced me to face the inevitable reality of my own nightmare.

I decided to launch a personal investigation to ascertain if this sheriff's behavior was an isolated incident or if it actually portrayed a fair representation of the old guard's behavior. The answer to that question would eventually force me to launch a search for my kidnapper.

I did not have to search very far for the first answer. Other law enforcement officials in adjoining counties provided more than enough additional insight. As constables in the forties, they had not acquired their skill through schooling. The lessons they learned came by following the example of others before them. It came as no surprise that there were generations of law enforcement people who had shared similar principles in conducting their business. And although the code to "protect and to serve" was not much different from today, the similarity ended there. The pursuit of their code was at whatever the cost. And sometimes the end justified the means for them. The "rights of the individual" were reserved for the innocent, not the guilty.

I can recall a conversation with a law enforcement officer at the lockup in St. Cloud. He expressed some confusion as to how the recent Supreme Court decisions might affect his operation. Specifically, he wanted to know if, under the new laws, a criminal had the right for an attorney to be present every time physical force was administered.

His question sounded so absurd, I thought at first he was joking. My response was that the basic legal right to have an attorney had nothing to do with the option of using physical force. I went on to make it clear that the law prohibited any use of physical force at any time unless the individual was endangering persons or property.

This particular law enforcement officer slowly brought his hand to his mouth to hide the wide grin growing across his face. I clearly got the impression that he figured *I* was joking. He replied, "I can't believe the courts would have gone that far."

I didn't have the heart to tell him that they had gone a whole lot farther than he would ever understand or be willing to accept.

From what I discovered in learning the history of the old guard, physical force had always been a crucial weapon in their arsenal to battle crime. Just as good old-fashioned common sense had made them street smart, their physical enforcement system had worked for years. Now the general consensus was that the new laws would bind their hands. In the end, it could only serve to free the criminals. In some ways they were correct. The clash of the two entirely different ideological worlds would require time to evolve.

Sitting alone in my law office that evening, I began to reflect on the question of what might have happened to my abductor so many years ago. Was he still alive? Was justice ever served? Why did I never have to go to court? The answers were even more elusive in light of how law enforcement of that period had administered their legal responsibilities.

I was also mindful of the fact that no family member had ever mentioned my abduction in all these years. In truth, the whole episode had been made to vanish as though it had never occurred. My unanswered questions set the stage for my mind to explore a whole avenue of intriguing thoughts.

History echoed the plight of our country in the 1940s. We were a nation overwhelmed in fighting a fierce and vicious war to preserve our way of life. For those in Washington engaged in this global battle to save the free world from total destruction, the standing order of the day was clear. We were to win at "whatever the cost." And for fifty-five million individuals, the final cost of World War II would be the sum total of everything they were or would ever be.

Within that context, it was understandable and inevitable that small communities on the prairie and across America formulated a similar mind set as to how to provide for their own protection and security. And how well each community survived became dependent on a form of justice that proclaimed that the end could sometimes justify the means.

Ultimately, from my research, I discovered that the responsibility to carry out that form of justice rested upon the shoulders of the local law enforcement. They were unofficially proclaimed as the communities' undisputed protectors. And to that end, they alone carried the burden to insure our freedom to live without fear.

In contrast, what I remembered about my abductor was that he had been more than just a common carnie from the circus. He was a malicious and undisciplined drifter who proved to be in every respect a dangerous predator to the well being of everyone in the community and especially to children.

In appearance, he may have looked like any ordinary man, but his intentions and heinous behavior were anything but ordinary. He did not abide by the same rules of moral conduct mandated by the community. On the contrary, he lived by his own immoral set of standards.

His sick fantasies were lewd and vicious. His presence invoked the question as to where on God's earth men like him could live among decent law-abiding folks. The taking of an innocent child from the sanctuary of his own home for self-gratification could only be viewed as an extreme violation in any code of decent behavior.

Furthermore, the man's deplorable behavior presented other serious concerns. For instance, had he assaulted or murdered other innocent children? If so, how many remained buried in unknown graves? And if he were ever released from jail, what would be the fate of other children? Could such a person ever change his behavior?

Answers to these troubling questions must have weighed heavily upon a constable bound to protect and serve. As the town guardian, he stood alone with only his badge for guidance and comfort. Tormented with the possibility that the lives of other innocent children under his protection might suffer a torturous death had to have been an agonizing burden to bear.

In the world of criminology as a defender and sometimes prosecutor, I shared an insight into the unwritten and unspoken policy to transport undesirables to the county line or beyond. However, this carnival man was more than just undesirable. He was much more than a nuisance; he was a threat. Viciously dangerous, he preyed upon the innocence of the very young. And although transporting a known criminal to another county may have protected one constable's community, he would, also, assume the responsibility for what course of events may happen next.

From what I had learned working closely with law enforcement, an officer's unwritten code of honor would have prevented him from doing anything to threaten the safety and security of another community. That silent bond of trust shared among brothers in law enforcement was as deep and sacred then as it is now. It was a bond forged by an understanding spirit that places the importance of another above oneself.

Several years would pass before that same unresolved question forced me to make a second examination into the ultimate disposition of my kidnapper. For the first time, I was compelled to return to the scene of the crime. I needed to research whatever records might still be available. Years of courtroom experience had mandated my need to discover the facts.

They say a good lawyer is a good fact finder. If correct, then I needed to uncover the facts that could place me in touch with the state of things as they actually existed when I was kidnapped. Unfortunately, my experience in the courtroom had also revealed that facts alone were not always conclusive truth or justified the justice that followed.

Robert Frost expressed a belief that, "A jury consists of twelve persons chosen to decide who has the best lawyer." There is a strong element of validity to his statement.

Richard Quinlivan, attorney in St. Cloud, had his own view of the legal justice system. Richard and his brother John were highly respected civil litigators. Retained by insurance companies, both had earned the reputation of being very challenging courtroom attorneys.

Like every new initiate to the practice of law, I had to earn people's respect. My partner, Paul Flora, engaged the

Quinvilans on many occasions. This future District Court judge was also revered among his peers. As for the young, long-haired new comer, it took the Bobick case to cross the bridge to reach Richard. He and Judge Rosengren were urging me to settle an injury case. Together they exerted a lot of pressure by asserting that my inexperience was going to cost my clients. Nevertheless, I stood my ground

I was somewhat concerned by this but took comfort in knowing that the Bobick family came from a line of fighters. I was told the older Bobick had fought Joe Lewis. A second Bobick had a reputation of fighting in and out of the ring. I had defended him as well, but not in a civil case. Fortunately, the jury sided against the insured defendant.

After that episode, I asked Richard if he ever felt guilty trying to champion a case not deserving of winning. Richard loved to offer up stories and bits of wisdom. My favorite was, "Never get into a pissing contest with a skunk because there are no winners, only losers."

In response to my question, he shared what another attorney had told him when he was younger. Apparently, the older lawyer had also been a successful litigator. When asked if he ever felt guilty winning so many jury trials, his response was no. He went on to explain that as an inexperienced trial lawyer, he lost fifty percent of the cases he should have won. Now as an experienced trial lawyer, he wins fifty percent of the cases he should not have won. So in the end, it all works out to be pretty much an even fifty-fifty.

Frost and Quinlivan were both correct. Trial by a jury has and will always remain an unpredictable form of justice. The rule of thumb was that if an attorney had a bad case with little evidence, he had a much better chance of winning with a jury.

I tried to imagine myself on a Grand Jury to determine whether sufficient facts warranted the trial of a constable involved in the disappearance of my alleged kidnapper. There was no statute of limitations on death cases, and the constable might have had more than just a helping hand in the fate of my abductor.

To establish a *prima facie* case, the prosecution outlined some of the information I had found in my own research. Some of the evidence would be factual. Other evidence would remain circumstantial because there were no eyewitnesses to the crime and no "*corpus delicti*," meaning "body relating to the crime." In legal jargon, there would be no direct proof that could establish the fact to any degree of absolute certainty.

What the jury would be offered was what the legal system refers to as "circumstantial evidence." That can be defined as indirect, secondary evidence from which a principal fact may be *reasonably* inferred legally. In layman's terms, the jury would be asked to give its best judgment if the facts appeared to be reasonable. And if those facts were reasonable, the jury might be able to rely upon them as a matter of fact. In this case, circumstantial evidence included:

1) The last known individual to ever see the victim alive was the constable.

2) Severe physical force had been administered to the kidnapper while in the custody of the constable.

3) That said force was not the result of an attempted escape or endangerment to others.

4) No known criminal charges for kidnapping or attempted murder were ever filed in the county court despite an abundance of evidence for prosecution.

5) The constable's close relationship with the boy's grandfather could have provided a motive. He had recently officiated as a pallbearer at his funeral.

6) Statements made by the constable, "That is all we need to know," and by the boy's father to the mother "that

everything had been taken care of" were consistent with a reasonable probability that a crime may have been committed.

7) The constable had opportunity. No one had access to the prisoner but the constable. In addition, city pay vouchers disclosed that the accused was paid on a regular basis to incinerate trash at the community dump. During each burn, no person other than the constable was permitted access to the area. It was an undisputed fact that the heat in these burns was so intense that everything, including dead carcasses of animals, was completely incinerated, leaving no physical evidence of ever existing. The accused had the perfect mechanism and opportunity to dispose of the *corpus delicti* (body of the crime). The ashes would tell no story.

8) One final note, the District Court Administrator advised that he was unable to locate the criminal files pertaining to this time period from the Court's archives. They had been either removed or misplaced.

What would be the final verdict? What legal course did justice eventually take? We will never be certain. In all likelihood, the final verdict may have been rendered by a judicial system without a judge or jury. Perhaps, jurisprudence was embodied within the rule of one man. If so, that rule of law had one single objective: to protect. I often wondered if the outcome would have been any different if Grandfather still had been constable.

It would be easy to rush to judgment and suggest vigilante law. But what if justice in the 1940s did not require proof beyond a reasonable doubt to know that ridding the world of a vicious predator preying upon children was reasonably necessary? One needs to be careful before making any rush to judgment. The law and justice have at times been peculiar bed fellows. They sometimes have a way of changing color like a chameleon depending on what bed of truth they decide to lie in.

The O.J. Simpson case revealed to the public this elusive secret of judiciousness that many practitioners have always known and quietly accepted. The jury had a once-in-a lifetime opportunity to tip the scales of justice the other way. And they made it happen. In hindsight, justice has often come in a variety of recipes the taste of which was dependent on who one was. Most people back in the 1940s just didn't know about this.

My own enlightenment came as a practicing attorney after nine years in the criminal justice system. Over those years, it became clearer that the principles of fairness and righteousness were more often in the eyes of the beholder than the blindfolded lady holding the scales of justice equally balanced. Those who meted out that justice were not always blind to their own principles of impartiality and equality. Rather, they were often helpless to the power of the other golden rule that stated, "Those who have the gold, rule."

Equally disturbing were other surprising revelations that unveiled the distorted world of the criminal. One in particular was painfully disturbing. In almost every instance I discovered that, if my client had been caught in one act of crime, there were often thirty others about which the system would never become aware.

For example, take the extreme case that involved a twenty-two-year old charged with a single burglary. Off the record, he admitted to one hundred fifty burglaries. Because of attorney privilege, the District Court judge would never be made aware of those other one hundred forty-nine crimes. Consequently, the defendant was given a light sentence to probation as a first-time offender. As for pedophiles, it is estimated that when placed on probation, they will average sixteen sexual assaults on children before being caught again. One of the problems with being a public defender was that I often felt I was on the wrong side.

Knowing what I had learned, there has never been any doubt in my mind that the kidnapper from the carnival had taken the lives of other children before he was finally caught. As a nameless pedophile, he traveled from state to state, never stopping for any period of time in any given location. The traveling circus provided the perfect cover for his criminal endeavors. Children were his specialty in a profession of surreal passion.

One has to get an overview of a child predator before one can begin to understand why these sick individuals do what they do. Their peculiar behavior is more than just a habit. It is an obsessive compulsion. Propelled by this relentless motivation, they pursue a passion that craves the use of children for their own pleasure. When finished, they kill them to avoid prison. It is a lesson acquired by experience and from other predators in the profession. Educated at Prison University, some have learned: no body, no crime.

The history of these pathetic careers can be overwhelming. They worship their passion as though it were a god. As the unspoken serial killers of the vulnerable and innocent, we house them in a criminal justice system that can never deter their unprincipled obsession. And when the judicial system tosses them back out on the street, which happens repeatedly, the cycle continues. Inevitably, somewhere, another family's child will be sentenced to death. Why? Were the Bill of Rights embodied in the Constitution intended to exclude children? Of course not, and if the law can protect the rights of the criminal, surely we can pass laws that will protect the innocent.

Aside from my own kidnapping ordeal, I believe every mom or dad at one time or another has experienced a moment when their child wandered away or could not be immediately located. When that happens, it is only natural for us to fear the possibility that our child could have been abducted. If more parents had any inkling on how many of these predators are out there, and how the justice system has been unable to protect their children, they would be even more frightened.

For those reasons, when my own children were born, I vowed that they would never be taken away by anyone. Yet, as hard as I endeavored to keep that promise, such an incident could have easily occurred with our son. It happened at the Sport Show in Minneapolis. My wife and I were working a display booth to promote our new summer horse camp. We were reaching out to children who wanted to experience a real outdoor adventure from the Old West.

We called our camp the Little Elk Ranch. It was situated on 1,200-plus acres of rolling woodlands, spring-fed lakes, and a virgin white pine forest hundreds of years old. The creation of the horse camp was my way to share the beauty and the natural adventures of the land as I had experienced them in my youth. Campers were outfitted with their very own horse for the entire week, provided by the ranch. A thousand young people came from all over the country each summer to ride scenic trails, learn horsemanship in the arenas and participate in camp-outs, water activities, crafts, sports, and a whole lot more.

On the weekends of the Sports Show, the Minneapolis Civic Auditorium attendance would easily exceed 20,000 a day. With so many people, we took special measures to insure that our three-year-old son, J. Christopher, was always safely tucked within his playpen at the rear of the booth.

On one of those weekends, in the midst of a capacity crowd, the unspeakable happened. J. managed to vanish. One minute he was asleep in the playpen; the next minute he was gone. As we began our frantic search, it was all I could do to keep my thoughts clear. Etched in my mind was the memory of my own abduction and the commitment that nothing like that would ever happen to our children. Now I could not escape the fear that our boy might have fallen into the hands of another such stranger.

The anguish of the moment brought an unexpected revelation of what my father must have experienced when he reported to the fire station on the day his son had been abducted. The shock and anger would have been immense. Once again, life was being measured in a matter of minutes. But I already knew time was not an ally as I charged back and forth searching through the crowd.

Rounding the corner, I spotted the flowing motion of the escalator carrying people to the second level. It was the same escalator we had ridden several times together prior to the show opening to the general public. Quickly, I reversed direction and pushed through the crowd towards the moving stairs. Sure enough, standing alone in the crowd by one of the guard rails, our son stood oblivious to his precarious circumstances.

As I gazed down, I could not help but notice some of his small features I had taken for granted. Features like the curly blond hair draping over his hazel-colored eyes, and that innocent childish grin radiating from his face. Kneeling down with arms outstretched, I enveloped him, and his small frame crumbled into my arms. I held him close much like the constable had once done with me many years ago.

J. Christopher had tempted fate and survived. For a brief moment, I pictured in my mind how relieved the constable must have felt when he sensed the miracle of life stirring within the little boy he cradled. If he was listening at that moment, I whispered a thought from my heart that he would always be a hero to me.

Over the years, the painful memory of the day I lost hope would find a way to personify itself over and over again. I can still remember working with Dad every summer to finish the electrical requirements for the carnival. Designated as the official electrical contractor for the fairgrounds, he was responsible for installing the temporary lighting and electrical connections. It was a substantial responsibility, requiring several weeks of work prior to opening night.

After the hard day's work was complete, I inevitably became involved in several physical fights with carnival youngsters. Normally due to my small size, I avoided physical confrontations. But for reasons unknown to me back then, I found a certain degree of satisfaction in these face-to-face fist fights with "carnies." I realize now that this physical interaction with carnival kids was part of a process for me to release the hostility I still carried towards my carnival abductor. However, before I had reached my teens that antagonism had disappeared.

One emotion would remain constant forever—I never cried again. During the period of this chapter in my life, I would be shot, battered by stones, smashed in the face, but nothing would bring a tear. Another quirk related to the abduction began after I was married. I would have dreams that my wife might someday be abducted.

The same was true when our children were born. The dreams were because my love for them was everything I was, and a part of me was still the little boy with a lingering memory. But the most haunting image was in the knowledge that they too might someday be looking over their shoulder hoping for me to appear.

Regrettably, for many families that nightmare of losing a child has become all too real. Even from within our small communities, we can discover those who have been taken away and are never found. Jodi Huisentruit was born in our community. Older when abducted by a predator, she was a vibrant young woman with a passionate exuberance for life and people. Now her fate has become shrouded in hushed obscurity and only the memory of the good can bring comfort to her mother, Jane, other family, and close friends.

The tragic abduction of a young boy riding his bicycle with his friends in another small community nearby was a second reminder that touched me deeply. His name was Jacob Wetterling. For him, another predatory stranger had appeared out of nowhere and abducted him in plain view of his playmates just as I had been taken. However, unlike myself, years have passed by, and Jacob has never returned or ever been found.

The Bridge of Hope is a lasting memory of an abduction, but it has another meaning for a survivor taken by a sexual predator.

A new bridge constructed over the Mississippi River north of St. Cloud was dedicated to the memory of his abduction. Appropriately, the memorial was named the Bridge of Hope. The curators of the memorial had an unrelenting desire to keep the memory of Jacob alive.

They were resolved to let the world know that they would not lose hope in their faith to eventually find Jacob, even though the possibility of a positive outcome was unlikely. Like hundreds of other parents, the outcome has always remained difficult to accept as they experience a lifetime in quiet tears.

In contrast, whenever I cross the bridge on my way to work at the Log Bank in St Cloud, the green sign with the word "HOPE" highlighted in white letters arouses a different remembrance. For those of us who have been abducted and survived, the four letters embody a different meaning. The word is synonymous with life as we recall how desperately we held on to a hope that a loved one would miraculously appear to deliver us from our frightening dream.

It was a hope tethered in a precarious balance between life and death. In the end, that expectancy of salvation ultimately became our only hope. For too many, it would become their last hope, as life disintegrated into a lonely and unknown grave.

# CHAPTER TWO

# A DOG'S TALE

LIKE MANY FAMILIES in small, rural communities, we enjoyed the companionship of a family dog. Why Mom and Dad invariably selected a small Boston terrier was never clear. Perhaps their decision had to do with family tradition. Then again, it may have been related to my small physique or our limited housing accommodations. For whatever the reason, a small terrier was definitely not my preference. After all, to a boy who spent ninety percent of his waking hours in the outdoors with illusions of being Tarzan or

Rodger at the age of four with one of several small Boston terriers that joined the family over the years.

another John Wayne, no small, yapping, foot-heeler, that at best chases squirrels, could ever be a dog of choice. I wanted something larger, more dramatic, or, failing that, at least more useful to me with illusions of being the "great hunter."

In the fall of 1949, against all my expectations, my world in the wild was abruptly interrupted by the introduction of school. Country-born children may have delighted in the opportunity to escape the many chores of farming, but for me, school had all the makings of a miserable form of confinement.

With doors closed and every window shut tight, how could a person be expected to hear the birds sing or smell the fragrances of nature floating on an afternoon breeze? Furthermore, expectations of sitting still within the confines of a small wooden cell for a whole day or raising one's hand in front of girls for permission to use the bathroom were even more concerning. Nevertheless, Mom and Dad made it very explicit. School was inevitable. But what happened along the way would capture the heart and soul of a little boy for a lifetime.

Reluctantly, on that first day of school, I began my "trail of tears" to the grade school. Most of me just wanted to vanish into the country landscape. With no intention of arriving before the first bell, I meandered through a series of backyards where only a month earlier trees where filled with scrumptious apples and plums ready for the taking. As I rounded a corner to an extended garage in the alley near the Blackhawk Cafe, my eye caught the sudden movement of a black streak. Instantaneously, barking as loud and furious as the crack of thunder in a summer rainstorm stopped me in my tracks. My breath froze as a huge black canine flung his body against a thin wire fence barely separating him from me and almost certain death.

Like a massive grizzly bear reared up on its hind legs, the dog towered over my small body by more than two feet. He must have outweighed my forty-pound frame by at least seventy pounds. Face to face his pearly white fangs behind snarling lips were more than just intimidating; they were down right terrifying.

Uncertain whether to run or hold still, instinctively my hand reached into my brown paper lunch sack and pulled out a sandwich. Mom insisted her young adventurer bring something substantial and healthy to school for noon lunch. Without hesitation, I tossed half of my double bologna, cheese, lettuce, and mayonnaise sandwich over the fence. The monster canine sprang high into the air, seizing the prize. As soon as all fours hit ground, he gulped down that half of my sandwich. I hated those mushy-tasting baloney sandwiches even more than the gagging consistency of my breakfast oatmeal or, worse yet, Cream of Wheat.

Without a qualm, I tossed the remaining portion of my noon lunch over the fence. While the dog ate that, I continued on my way. Shaken but no longer frighten, the exhilaration from the surprise encounter had illuminated into an awesome and unforgettable memory. I think it was the dog's sheer power that thrilled me. Here was an animal worthy of my imagination.

As for school, it lived up to every gloomy expectation. Cloakrooms intended for hanging garments also served as solitary confinement for anyone who over-exercised his freedom of speech. The principal in charge of our educational future also functioned as a no-pardon warden with corporal punishment authority. In the classroom, my first teacher seemed bound and determined to improve our hearing by stretching our ears. Whenever one spoke out of turn or violated a rule, she was quick to yank on an ear.

Aside from recess, the only classroom exercise depended on how often one could sharpen a pencil before being rebuked by

Old Ironsides. Perched on an elevated platform in front of the classroom, she constantly scanned the room with piercing eyes. They had the power to stare holes through anything, much like Flash Gordon's ray gun, but not nearly as much fun.

Fortunately, for those of us who had the capacity to daydream, nothing remained impossible, nor too far away to reach with a little imagination. Teacher would sometimes comment, "Rodger, you are not going to get anywhere dreaming out the window."

She did not know that, without dreams, life would never be more than it seemed. Her favorite saying was, "If the shoe fits, put it on." It was hard to imagine that first graders were ready for a course in philosophy. Nevertheless, she repeated that phrase over and over again. It must have made her feel good about something.

As for me, the irresistible magnetism of that powerful, majestic dog pulled my thoughts away from everything except the memory of my encounter with him. I could not help but fantasize what it would be like to actually own such a courageous canine.

Over the ensuing months, the bond that the dog and I shared with a sandwich developed into a special relationship. Every morning on the way to school I gifted him with Mom's carefully prepared lunch. Excited by my offerings, this dog of my dreams raced around the pen doing his best to entertain me by sitting up, jumping, and even making 360-degree turns on command.

By the time the first year of school rolled by, the two of us had become the best of friends. Yet, a certain degree of apprehension always remained. This was, after all, a truly powerful, potentially dangerous animal. I called him "Blackie." The name immortalized our first meeting when this black, explosive force almost turned me into a ghost before my time.

In spite of our affectionate relationship over the ensuing months, I did not forget that our friendship never extended beyond the protective fence that separated us. His superior size and strength were more of a challenge than my small first-grade physique could ever hope to handle.

Dogs have always had an uncanny way of seeing the best in people. For that reason, they seem to have an innate instinct as to whom they chose to befriend. For as long as history can remember, canines have shared a special kinship with mankind. As for Blackie, the enthusiasm for our relationship was noticeable whenever I entered the premises. In fact, he became so excited that his whole body trembled as though the earth were moving beneath his feet.

As the school year came to a close, the bond between dog and boy had evolved into a secret alliance. But before the tolling of the last bell that year, an incident occurred that would change our lives forever.

After a long nine months, the end of May brought happy days again as the sweet sound of the final bell to dismiss everyone for the summer began ringing. As I passed through the double doors of the grade school, it was a beautiful sunny day. Patches of sunlight beamed through the trees and danced on the ground along with children jumping and shouting for joy. The yellow country buses already lined the street for a block waiting for the final good-byes to be shared.

As I began my own journey across the schoolyard, my mind had already turned to thoughts of the exciting adventures waiting to be exploited in the three long months ahead of me. I could hear the land and the distant rivers calling me home. However, one adventure I did not envision. Blackie sat on the curb across the street.

I froze in disbelief. Then my legs kicked into overdrive as I darted off like a rabbit. When Blackie spotted me, he leaped from the curb and charged towards me like a express train. To elude his oncoming charge, I dashed into the intersection just ahead of the parked school buses, but it was to no avail. The black shadow streaked out of nowhere, and we collided. Tumbling, we fell to the pavement into a mass of tangled bodies.

When we stopped rolling, my face was pressed flat to the pavement, my entire body held rigid. Blackie, on the other hand, full of exuberance, instantly rose to his feet, panting and drooling. Then with a gentle tongue, he began to lick my arm and cheek. As I peeked from beneath my arms, I recognized that familiar, friendly trademark. His big wooly tail wagged so vigorously that his large frame was set to swaying. Just when I was certain that our friendship endured without the fence between us, Blackie stiffened and sounded a deep growl. I had not heard that threatening sound since the first day we met.

Whether it was the memory of that first day or my precarious circumstances, every muscle in my body again froze. A noisy crowd of children, bus drivers, and teachers, who had witnessed Blackie's flying tackle of a first-grader, came running. The afternoon breeze that once carried the joyful sounds of children was now replaced by the frantic sounds of screaming and yelling.

Unbeknown to me, those assembling mistakenly assumed that the large black canine had launched a savage attack on the little boy lying in the street. As good Samaritans, they were rushing forward to my rescue. With all the clamor and semblance of people attacking, Blackie's demeanor instinctively transformed from one of extreme jubilation to that of ferocious defender. His head began to dart in every direction as hairs bristled across the back of his huge frame now trembling uncontrollably over me.

The drama rapidly deteriorated into a showdown between good and supposed evil. Like a Hollywood western, each side squared off in the middle of the city street waiting for one or the other to make the first move.

Unfortunately, the perception as to who was good or evil was pretty murky. What no one in the crowd understood was that, unlike human nature, the dog had no premeditated reason to cause harm. Nevertheless, a skirmish line of would-be rescuers surrounded me and my would-be defender, cutting off any avenue of escape. As for Blackie, he squared himself over my body with no notion that he was merely surrounded by rescuers rather than dangerous adversaries intent on doing me harm. By the same token, the crowd lacked the capacity to grasp that Blackie, had not harmed me, had no intention of doing so, and was merely responding in self-defense.

Before anyone could bring the two worlds back into harmony, a young man advanced from within the crowd. He carried a bat held high in the air. No doubt, his intentions were to scare or intimidate Blackie. But as the man approached, Blackie firmly held his ground. His vocal chords began to grumble a deep, rumbling growl, as he slowly crouched even lower to the pavement over my body.

When the young man advanced within a few feet of us, Blackie exploded with the force of a small bomb, leaping into the air like a leopard. His lunge was quick and decisive. With no forewarning, the man was caught completely off guard. Unbalanced, he stumbled backward to the pavement with a 100 pounds of black fury attached to his chest.

As a piercing shriek echoed down the line of buses, panic broke out along the street. Screaming spectators began to push and shove in every direction, desperately trying to escape the fury unleashed by Blackie. The shuffling sound of footsteps scrambling in retreat signaled a high point in crowd hysteria. From within the turmoil, two older men cautiously advanced to assist the injured young man who had fallen into a crumbled heap next to the curb.

In the blink of an eye, Blackie had forced the aggressor to the ground, delivered a slashing gash and retreated to a protective stance over my body. Standing alone against the entire world, the odds were against him. The numbers before him were not in his favor. He may not have wanted a confrontation, but he had been dealt a hand with no other choice.

Those who have observed a rabbit like a snowshoe or cottontail confronted with danger in the wild know that the rabbit's first instinct is to remain perfectly motionless. He has learned through evolution that a predator cannot harm that which he cannot see. Following the rabbit's instinct, my response had been the same. With no place to hide, I had chosen to remain motionless in a desperate attempt to become invisible to my own danger.

It would be years before I could piece together the entire drama behind Blackie's extraordinary actions on that day. Thanks to his owner and thirty-five subsequent years of close ties to many generations of my own Labradors since that day, I eventually understood the deep relationship between man and dog. With divine devotion that transcends all other sentiments, the Labrador is the embodiment of a spiritual passion that will always inspire loyalty and sacrifice.

Dogs are descendants of wolves whose instinct for preservation has been cultivated and perfected over thousands of years under extreme conditions. Yet, they also acquired a gentler side. Caring for family and other members in the pack, they evolved a sixth sense that enabled them to feel, understand and react to expressions made by others rather than just themselves.

More important, every dog is a distinct individual with different personal characteristics much like us. They are intelligent and can learn from schooling. And, yes, I believe they even dream. They often express emotions of love, joy, and sadness. But to communicate with them, one needs to learn their language. Understanding a dog's mind is like learning any foreign language. In the beginning, the context of their lingo may seem awkward. But once you begin to grasp meaning from their gestures, temperament, and other responses, communication is inevitable.

The emotional true story of the "Dog's Tale" was a drama of tenacious courage and unwavering loyalty. Unlike a movie script, it did not have a predetermined beginning and ending. Rather it evolved through a series of emotional interactions that transcended the characteristic barriers separating man from animal.

Picture the feeling of that last day of a school year in the eyes of a youngster. All the excitement and anticipation of a seemingly endless summer floods one's thoughts as the child anxiously awaits the final bell to ring. From within the stuffy confinements of the classroom, the warm sun and the smells of summer beckon one to escape into the world of play. No more homework, no more rules, and no more confinement—the luxury of freedom is only minutes away.

For Blackie, this was also a special day. The latch on his kennel had been left open. His freedom was also at hand. The unexpected opportunity opened a whole new world of adventure beyond his enclosure. Some how Blackie managed to find his way to the school premises. Perhaps it was by accident. Or, he may have been following one of many mothers walking in that direction to pick up their children on that last day of school. Perhaps he actually followed my scent.

Whatever drove him, he found himself sitting on the corner across the street from the schoolyard just as I came out.

Maybe he enjoyed the happy sounds of children playing, reminding him of his young friend. Perhaps he considered the possibility that his friend might be somewhere among the children. Maybe he knew I was. And, even before he saw me, he reveled in the idea of us playing together with no fence as a hindrance. Certainly, the very notion of such a possibility caused the rush of excitement that precipitates a sudden muscle contraction.

Prone to daydreaming from many hours of confinement, Blackie's thoughts might have drifted to the times spent with the boy. He was reminded of how wonderful that feeling was when a child and a dog shared special time together. Each was inherently capable of communicating joy and longed for a period of timeless affection. Though he may not have understood all I told him, he knew I loved him. Maybe he could see it in my eyes or hear it in the soft way I spoke to him. I know he enjoyed the treats I shared. For Blackie affection had a way of expressing itself in more than words.

The view Blackie had as he watched the children play near the front entrances to the school.

Treasuring these fond memories, his thoughts might have shifted into the opposite direction. Maybe he has been too quick or too eager to share the boy's food. After all, Sarge, his owner who has been like a father to him, had always provided ample food in his special bowl. As attention drifted to his life with Sarge, Blackie might have sensed another surge of warm feeling gelling. He could fondly have recalled how Sarge had taught him everything he knew. And maybe he was reminded of the many exciting adventures the two of them had shared traveling around the territory, especially their hunting.

As he continued his vigilance over the schoolyard, it became clear that Sarge and his young friend measured the two most important relationships in his life. There was nothing he would not sacrifice for either one. However, the boy was different. Blackie recalled that special feeling whenever his little hand brushed gently against the end of his soft nose through the fence. And whenever the boy bounced in and out of the yard, his exuberance was captivating. Just watching the lively spirit in action reminded him of the happy days when he was a puppy. Perhaps Blackie began to fantasize on the similarities the two of them had in common. Especially how they shared a kindred spirit personified in an unwavering bond of trust.

Blackie's thoughts might have continued to meander when, to his surprise and delight, his friend unexpectedly exits the front door. As the boy strolled onto the lawn, Blackie rose jubilantly to his feet. His tail began its salutation. Unconsciously, his feet began to prance nervously in place. When the temptation to run was no longer controllable, he sprinted to the boy in long strides like a greyhound giving chase. Filled with exhilaration, he could hardly wait for the moment when he could reach out and lick his friend with love and affection.

When he approached the boulevard, his friend made a sharp turn and raced toward the street. To Blackie, the notion of playing tag was too tempting. Quickly, he seized an opportunity to take a short cut through the buses. In one quick breath, he closed the distance near the intersection in front of the leading school bus. With one final leap, he tagged his friend. As they collided, they fall to the pavement where their bodies begin tumbling like autumn leaves blowing in a prairie wind.

Blackie eagerly jumped to his feet to pursue the game. But, the boy remained motionless. Blackie might have considered that something was wrong. Was his friend hurt in the fall, or did he just want to play another game? As Blackie reached out with affectionate licks to encourage his friend, his eyes turn towards the onslaught of a crowd of hostiles yelling and making threatening gestures.

They were charging towards him and his friend. Canine senses originating from times long before dog and man were friends, signaled an alert to defend against imminent harm. Instinctively his hair began to stiffen along with his courage. Conscious of the unspoken bond to protect, he positioned himself directly over the body of his fallen friend.

As the crowd converged dangerously close, Blackie snarled a warning to keep their distance. Sensing no response, he inhaled an even deeper breath and delivered a loud, menacing snarl that demanded respect. Confronted with a pair of fiery eyes backed by a hundred pounds of black muscle ready to attack, the message was finally acknowledged.

Wary of Blackie's intentions, the intruders began to form a tight perimeter. The prospect of entrapment probably did not go unnoticed as Blackie unleashed an even more menacing growl backed by a storming charge when someone got too close. The skirmish line responded, rolling in a backward motion. The aggressiveness of his attack brought tensions to a new height. But the crowd had not dispersed, and deep inside, Blackie might have begun to sense that threats alone would not be enough.

If circumstances required a fight to the end, his resolve would not be deterred. Abandoning his friend was not an option. As Blackie's eyes glared down the enemy, a man with a large stick moved away from the protection of the crowd. Blackie heard the man shout, "I'm going for the boy." The words maybe had no particular meaning to Blackie, but the tone of his voice suggested that the crisis was reaching a level of serious danger. Making a reassuring glance downward, he noticed his frightened friend had sought refuge by burying his face in his arms against the pavement.

The window of opportunity to avoid confrontation closed, and Blackie prepared to take aggressive action. His eyes fixed intensely on the man moving directly towards him and the boy. With every step Blackie's heartbeat quickened. Whatever action he was about to encounter, it would have to be quick and decisive. He would not leave his friend unprotected for any period of time.

Blackie's front paws begin to dig into the pavement as the man paused only a few steps away. When the aggressor slowly raised the wooden object high into the air, every muscle in Blackie's body experienced a series of twitches as though receiving jolts from an electric current. With a rattlesnake's timing and accuracy, he struck with lightning speed.

Flying through the air like a cannon ball, a hundred pounds of muscle and bone landed squarely upon the man's chest. Instantly, Blackie sank his fangs deep into the fleshly muscle of the man's upper arm. Then, with the grip of an iron vice, he crunched down with bone-breaking force.

So sudden was Blackie's explosive charge, the man had no chance to retreat. Caught in a title wave of black fury, he staggered backward and crashed to the pavement. As the wooden object dropped to the ground, the man screamed out in desperation. His cry of pain resonated through those gathered near enough to hear. Recognizing the sound of defeat, Blackie immediately withdrew.

Returning victorious to his friend, Blackie gave him an encouraging nudge with the butt of his soft nose. Nuzzling close, he tried to reassure his friend that everything was under control. Minutes later, he resumed his towering stance over the motionless body. With jaws clenched as a formidable defense, a mixture of dripping saliva and blood began to trickle to the pavement and eventually onto the boy.

Most disconcerting to Blackie was that, having tasted the blood of his enemy, he had changed in ways he could not explain. It was as though some long, forgotten instinct as ancient as the saber tooth tiger beckoned him to respond with more finality.

Meanwhile, beyond the inner circle of spectators, attention was focused on the injured man. For Blackie, the apparent lull in hostility provided a brief but needed rest. Exhausted, but determined to the end, Blackie reclined on the pavement, positioned close to his fallen friend. Crossing his fore paws he assumed the position characteristic of the breed when times are more calm and relaxed. And although Blackie remained vigilant, he still managed to nestle close enough so that the warmth of his presence could reassure his small friend.

However, the tranquility was short lived. From within the crowd, a second man advanced. This man, unlike the first, was older, more massive. Blackie perceived a threat of catastrophic proportions. He had no way to know that the man was a retired over-the-road trucker now driving a school bus. His massive size had more to do with weight than muscle.

But the mere appearance of super strength once again stirred a deep, ancestral instinct, demanding a more deadly response than his first. Trusting his instincts, Blackie prepared to lunge directly for the man's throat. His senses told him that there was no other alternative. He could no longer afford the luxury of hesitation or uncertainty.

Glancing nervously from side to side, the daunting challenge before him weighed heavily as he crouched low to the pavement. A strange and deathly silence hovered in the air. But inside Blackie, a volcanic tension waited to erupt as his front paws begin to scrape the pavement. His glazed eyes locked onto the silhouette approaching.

When the stench of the intruder reached Blackie's nose, it telegrammed the command to attack. Quicker than the eye could follow, Blackie catapulted into the air. The man only had enough time to twist his head to avoid an eyeball to eyeball confrontation. Fortunately for him, Blackie's fangs missed their intended target, though they manage to rip deep into the flesh of the man's left cheek. A resounding cry of anguish once more echoed throughout the block.

As Blackie prepared to make his second lunge, the man turned and scrambled along the curb to escape. Clutching one hand to the cheek bubbling over with blood, the man stumbled onto the boulevard and collapsed. Reaction to this second bloody attack created sheer panic. Hysterical people swarmed everywhere in the rush to disperse, like a school of minnows flashing away in response to an approaching net. Terrified, people begin stumbling to the ground, becoming themselves casualties. Some screamed while others embraced as though the end were near. For Blackie, the fear of Armageddon shifted the balance once more in his favor.

But no sooner did Blackie again return to the side of his fallen friend, the sound of a high-pitched siren came from down the street. Glancing over his shoulder, Blackie spotted the flashing lights racing in his direction. Too distant to be perceived as an immediate threat, Blackie settled down for a much-needed rest. When the strange object reaches the intersection, he watched a man stepping out of the vehicle. The stranger appeared to be someone of importance; he immediately took command of the intruders.

A remarkable event occurred. The man with the flashing lights on the car hood succeeded where Blackie had not. He forced everyone out of the street. As Blackie observed him, a calm descended. Help had apparently arrived. In a matter of minutes, children were moving onto the buses while others entered the school or simply departed all together.

Blackie continued his monitoring of the events surrounding his position. He could not help but notice that the man carried a long-barreled instrument. Blackie was familiar with such objects. Sarge always carried a similar object whenever they went hunting. Blackie knew they were most helpful in hunting birds.

For a moment, his canine mind was distracted. He began to wonder if game birds were nearby. Sniffing the air, he neither saw nor detected the scent of any game birds. Then again, how could he be sure of anything? After all, for the past hour he had been distracted in the protection of his friend.

From time to time, the strange man behaved as though he wanted to approach, but, he never intentionally walked too close, never posed a threat to which Blackie had to respond. When the man finally advanced forward a few steps, he crouched on one knee. Eye to eye, Blackie's interest was aroused. This was not aggressive behavior. Then the man raised the long-barreled object to his shoulder. As it pointed directly at Blackie, the man's intentions were not certain. Obviously, no birds were around. Face to face, Blackie was confused if the stranger was a friend or

THE BOY MY CHILDREN NEVER KNEW

foe.

Carefully the man leaned his head forward on the barrel. Never were the stakes so high. But the real consequences of a gun being fired or even death were not comprehensible to Blackie. In the evolution of things, he had not been equipped with the capacity to reason that lead could correlate with dead.

Before any final resolution was reached, an unexpected miracle appeared. Down the street, Blackie spotted a familiar black pickup slowly making its way towards the intersection. He immediately recognized the vehicle as belonging to Sarge. When it came to a halt and the driver's door squeaked opened, his beloved companion Sarge stepped from the cab.

Blackie could hardly control the sudden surge of emotion. For the first time, he sensed that everything was going to be just fine. Gleaming down at his friend on the pavement, he repeatedly barks out the good news, "We are safe. Sarge has come!" Yet his friend remained strangely quiet and unaffected by the good news.

When Sarge reached out his large calloused hand, it was a signal for Blackie to come. Blackie's response was one of elation as he rushed to embrace Sarge. After receiving a few gentle pats to the head and around the neck, Blackie stood at attention on all fours. He then led Sarge over to the boy. As Sarge knelt down to lift the little friend into his arms, he had already surmised in his heart what had happen.

With the protection of his little friend accomplished, Blackie pranced triumphantly to the pickup with the two most important people in his life near his side. Under the close scrutiny of Blackie, the boy was placed safely in the front seat. Sarge then lifted his longtime companion into the back of the truck. By now, Blackie found it very difficult to restrain his excitement. He began pacing the four corners of the box in anticipation of hearing the roar of the engine.

Before Sarge could depart, he has one more important commitment. Strolling over to the man with the gun, the two engaged in a quiet conversation, but Blackie was not concerned. He concluded that the man must have been a friend. Sarge was no doubt expressing his deep gratitude for the man's assistance in their rescue. When the conversation was finished, Sarge ambled over to Blackie and extended a comforting hand. Overjoyed, Blackie responded in a surge of caring licks.

Blackie loved riding in the pickup more than anything else except hunting. Stretching his head out beyond the cab, he turned his face directly into the wind. As the breeze brought a pleasant coolness, he closed both eyes to savor the moment.

When the pickup arrived at home, the boy was lifted from the front seat and carried into the house. To Blackie's surprise Sarge returned carrying his hunting gun. That could only mean one thing. They were going hunting! Blackie accepted this as a reward for his gallant behavior. Any previous notion of being tired quickly dissipated when Sarge opened the door of the cab to invite Blackie to join him.

As the two snuggle close on the front seat, Blackie was too excited to notice Sarge's unusual quiet. When the pickup approached an unfamiliar dirt road past the water tower, Blackie wondered if they had taken the wrong road. However, such concerns were quickly dismissed, for Sarge had never been lost.

On the edge of town past the grass runway of the airport, the road entered a forbidden landscape covered with bits and pieces of debris. Traveling over mounds of scattered junk, the pickup rolled to a complete stop. Blackie was certain that they have never hunted here before. Sarge opened the passenger door, and his lifetime companion bolted from the cab.

Irrespective of his bizarre surroundings, Blackie instinctively transformed into a fine-tuned hunting machine. With nose glued to the ground, he began to sniff for messages that would tell him if game was nearby. Right away his instincts began to signal that something was wrong. The ground smelled repugnant, and that familiar scent of wildlife was nowhere to be found.

After several minutes of intensive searching, Blackie was at a loss. He was not quite sure how to continue. Confused he returned to the pickup for further instructions. Bounding over a heap of garbage he was confident Sarge would have an answer. After all, Sarge raised him from a pup and taught him everything he knew. And, as a father and best friend, Blackie trusted Sarge without reservation. It was an enduring trust that had never failed.

Blackie reached the pickup, and he noticed that Sarge had never left the cab. Apparently, he remained behind watching his hunting companion making the rounds from the window. Tail wagging, Blackie anxiously waited by the door.

Sarge slowly stepped from the vehicle with gun in hand. He walked to the rear of the pickup. Resting the gun against the fender, he crouched down on both knees. Then, reaching out with both arms, he summons his beloved Blackie. As always, his best friend darted over to nuzzle a soft nose gently up against the side of his face. The exchange of soft strokes and gentle nudges was a display of man and dog at their very best. Sarge ended the face-to-face greeting with a long, tender embrace.

Standing up tall and straight, he shouted out the familiar command to make another run. Instantly, Blackie jumped to the occasion and sprinted off in a series of long leaps. As he hurdled a collection of cans, the sound of a single shot broke the silence. Blackie felt a burning in his side followed by a paralysis preventing any further movement. Without knowing why, his legs began to crumple beneath him. Just as he fell to the ground he caught a glimpse of Sarge rushing towards him.

Reaching his side, Sarge dropped to the ground to cradle Blackie's head in his arms. As Blackie strained to cuddle up close, his father's eyes absorbed in water did not go unnoticed. Blackie opened his mouth to speak, but no sound came out. He made a desperate effort to lick Sarge's hand, but the strength in his massive body was gone.

For reasons unknown to Blackie, only his eyes were able to communicate. But he was not concerned. Even without the slightest whisper, he knew he was telling Sarge how much he loved him. It was as though he were looking straight into his father's heart. Then, in a brief moment as Blackie gazed upon his loving image, the world around him slipped into darkness, and he passed forever into the never-ending dream world.

Over the years the memory and experiences of that day have played over and over in my mind. Blackie had been wrongfully branded a danger and sentenced to death. With his back to the wall, his fighting spirit to protect me could never be broken.

Foremost in Blackie's mind was his loyalty to me. It was an unwavering loyalty that would transcend his suffering. It came from an enduring bond that had been fine tuned from generations long ago. In the end, the real tragedy was ours alone, for those he loved and trusted the most could not save him.

The memory of what happened to Blackie would leave a profound personal legacy. And although I could not turn back the time to change the outcome, I could only look forward to keeping his memory alive. My decision to befriend and raise Labradors was a tribute to Blackie. My all time favorite movie was *Old Yeller*. And with each Labrador generation born, the spiritual bond between his descendants and the boy from the past was reunited over and over again.

One day many years later, a black Labrador wandered into my life. I often wondered if it was divine fate or mere coincidence that brought this orphaned dog into the family. Whatever the circumstances, I could not help but notice how much he reminded me of Blackie. Cast in an image of a most courageous male with no fear, he had a natural propensity to communicate with his chosen family. Of utmost significance was his undivided devotion to befriend and protect our four-year-old son. The dog's name was Racho. And like "Old Yeller," he, too, had been abandoned by someone and was in need of a new home. When we adopted Racho into the family, he responded in turn by adopting our son J. Christopher.

For Racho, ranch life in the open country could not have been more suitable. Roaming free without any boundaries seemed to be everything he ever wanted. Never looking back from wherever he had come, the bond between this dog and another little boy grew very strong. How strong would seriously be put to the test the day our son vanished.

It was late in the fall. Racho and J. played in the tall pine forest as his parents set about the task of raking tons of fallen leaves. As the hours passed by quickly, we had hardly given a thought to anything

J. and Racho had established an inseparable bond.

but the work we did. Living isolated and surrounded by a thousand acres of wilderness, the normal concerns of city life fell away. And with the addition of Racho, we took additional comfort in knowing we had a third parent to keep an eye on J.

When the decision was finally made to quit after a long, hard day of raking, we called out for J. But, in spite of our repeated calls, there was no response. We then proceeded to the house and searched every room. Still no luck. We even combed the large camp bunkhouse with no success. As we rounded the corner of the horse barn, we spotted Racho lying beneath the big oak tree. With fore paws crossed before him, he was relaxed, gazing off towards the lake. However, J. was nowhere in sight.

When we continued shouting for J. out over the hillcrest leading to the lake, Racho's attention was aroused. He raced to my side. With his tail swaying back and forth, he had that look that said, "What do you want?"

Insulated by its remoteness, the ranch landscape encompassed lakes, swamps, and several large tracts of forest that provided an endless assortment of beautiful scenery and much wildlife, but, in this situation, too many life-threatening scenarios. With desolation, I realized that the numbers of ways one so young as J. could disappear and not be discovered for a long time were extensive. We had no clue what direction our son may have decided to take in his wandering. With the sun creeping low on the horizon, the options before us were many, but time was short. Each trail, each direction would require hours to search, the kind of hours we could not afford as darkness comes early to the forest in the fall.

Minnesota has two different climactic conditions at this time of the year. Between sunrise and sunset the sun can bring the temperature up to a comfortable sixty-five degrees. Under the cover of darkness, however, the temperature can plummet to below freezing. J. was wearing nothing more than a short sleeve shirt and a pair of shorts. He might not survive a night in freezing temperatures. With the rapid loss of heat to an open sky, his small body would inevitably slide to a subnormal temperature. Technically referred to as hypothermia, this was a condition with which we, who resided in the far north, were very familiar.

Any expectation to recover our lost son in time now focused on Racho. I mentally weighed the possibility of whether that same deep bond Blackie had for me could be alive somewhere within Racho for J. If so, could it be aroused in time to bring back our son?

These were some very troubling questions that required a quick response. Dropping to both knees, I reached my arms out to Racho. With my hands on his shoulders, I began repeating over and over, "Find J.!" "Where's J.?" "Let's get J.!" "Go Racho. Fetch J.!"

The challenge was to make him understand that our son needed him now. He showed every appearance of understanding that there was urgency in my voice. If he knew what it was about, I could not be certain. But deep within his powerful chest, I could hear the rhythm of short murmuring sounds. His feet were prancing nervously in place. Suddenly, he broke away from my arms. With a surge of energy he charged off in the direction of the camp's recreation field.

We followed close behind. Being much faster, Racho would rush ahead, stop, look back and then anxiously stomp all four feet in one place until we closed the gap. Then once more he would dash off again. He continued to repeat the same process over and over again.

When we entered the recreation field near the pine forest, Racho was already cris-crossing the area, his nose to the ground. He appeared to be on some kind of a trail. What or who he was trailing still remained anyone's guess. Suddenly, he turned from the field and charged up the driveway. I didn't understand what he was doing or why he had made this abrupt change of direction. It was confusing. Did Racho even understand what was expected of him?

The answer to that question seemed to be clearly, no. Now, as he raced from the yard, he wanted us to follow him down the township road. To do so was against all the odds of logic. Jay at this very young age had never ventured out on the dirt road. It was a quarter of a mile from the house. It had no particular destination. The closest community was six miles away. Considering the many exciting destinations on the rest of the property, it was difficult to imagine why he would take this dusty road.

As we half-heartedly followed the dog, my mind debated whether to recall Racho and start over. But deep down, my heart trusted Racho's instincts. Some inborn premonition prevented me from abandoning that faith that Racho knew where J. could be found. As dusk turned the remaining twilight to darkness, that confidence proved to be correct. Reaching a rise in the road, we spotted in the distance the small silhouette of a child.

The divine sensation of finding our lost son was nothing less than a miracle. And in that brief moment, Racho was exalted and revered as the savior who had made it possible. How did Racho understand what we had expected from him? I like to believe the answer can be found somewhere within the life force of that inexorable bond between dogs and people.

It is a covenant defined by an unwavering loyalty that has been passed on from generation to generation by his kind. Something both primitive and instinctual, it creates a binding force as natural as that between a parent and a child. And, in the face of adversity, the bond will instinctively strengthen.

J. later revealed to his mother that he was on his way to

visit Grandma. At the tender age of four, he could not appreciate the fact that Grandma lived twelve miles away. J. did select the correct direction to begin his journey to Grandma. However, there were many other roads he would have had to know before he reached his destination. We knew the outcome of his adventure could have been tragic.

In my childhood, Blackie's special bond was an inspiration to protect the boy my children never knew. A generation later, another black Labrador's bond may have saved the life of another boy his children will never know. Call it a miracle, call it coincidental, call it luck, but on that day I put to rest any thought there would never be another Blackie. I had been wrong.

The enduring spirit of Blackie remains alive in the hearts of Labradors today and those yet to be born. And although Blackie may have breathed his last, many more just like him are out there waiting to be discovered. I, for one, will be forever indebted to his noble kind. For they have truly earned the reputation of being "man's best friend."

# CHAPTER THREE

# A COMMUNITY REMEMBERED

I N THE TIME PERIOD of my childhood, neighborhoods
thrived with their own defining character. While most
families were descendants from faraway places like
Norway, Sweden, and Germany, with honored ancestral tradi-
tions, they still expressed a strong sense of pride in their community. Blended together, they evolved collectively into their
own distinct generation of new Americans. All across America,
our time would also come to be known as the period of the
"common man myth."

Living in harmony, everyone shared an understanding
that life never provided any guaranties nor should it. Yet, the
collective strength of this new breed of Americans perpetuated
a belief that everything was possible. Horizons that might once
have appeared far away were now considered accessible. And
we who were born to that generation would inherit the legacy
and preservation of their American Dream.

As individuals, residents nurtured a general character
deeply rooted in peace and stability. They went about their
daily business with sincerity and a personal commitment to

improve their economic and social status. Yet, they were always careful to adhere to their own values of decency. Up early to meet life's challenges, they were pure in heart, tough and reserved. But above all their virtues, I relish most the memory of how they truly cared for each other, and how they found time to come together to share those feelings.

Every Friday evening, whether old or young, from town or country, visitor or resident, folks migrated to fill Main Street. Some simply relaxed in the comfort of a parked vehicle, savoring a favorite ice cream treat from the soda fountain in the drug store on the same block as the theater. Others strolled along the sidewalk, munching on a five-cent bag of popcorn from the little yellow stand in the park by the tracks. Many folks were simply standing in friendly clusters. To assure a favorite location, one had to arrive early before every available parking space was taken. By seven o'clock, it was difficult to negotiate space along the sidewalk.

They were eager to share the weekly gossip and converse about the weather with both friends and new acquaintances. The city band playing patriotic Sousa marches from the nearby park carried the mood of the evening on a fresh summer breeze. But it was the warm smiles on people's faces that revealed the joy in their hearts for each other's company.

Only the festivities of the summer fair surpassed this town camaraderie. The county fair was truly the grandest get-together of the year by any measurement. Excitement soared to epic heights for children to grandparents and from the casual onlooker to avid thrill seekers as they explored the animal barns and cruised the midway.

The fair coliseum, built in 1936, provided one of the largest and finest hardwood dance floors in the upper Midwest. For a short period in 1945 it housed German prisoners during

World War II. They were detained there specifically to help local farmers harvest their crops.

During the fair, the fancy coliseum was filled with the sights and fragrances of fresh flowers, tasty pastries, homespun apparel, and many other artistic exhibitions vying for a blue ribbon. With park benches inside and out, it was a perfect place to rest and converse with friends.

In contrast, the midway was jammed with a much younger crowd. Loud music intermingled with the constant chattering and screams of terror from the tilt-a-whirl or octopus. Beyond the noise, hawkers could be heard shouting, "Take home your own teddy bear" or "Win a prize every time."

But of all the exciting adventures, nothing could top the exalted Model-T races. Prior to every major performance at the grandstand, engines were cranked into action as the hearts of spectators soared. It was, by all accounts, the ultimate crowd pleaser. For many enthusiasts, missing this race would compare to an ardent football fan of today not seeing his favorite team as it played in the Super Bowl.

What made these events so popular was the expectation of the unexpected. The only limitation was imagination, and that was never in shortage. The Model-T racer itself had no outward framework. Stripped to a motor, gas tank, and a single seat attached to an iron frame, it could only be started by cranking a right-angled rod attached to the front of the engine. The entire assembly was never designed for looks, only for speed.

Prior to commencing the race, autos were placed along the starting line. Then the drivers made their way to the wooden stage platform before the grandstand. With crowds jamming the inside track and packing the grandstand where the contestants received their instructions, the air was electrified with excitement as the announcer described in detail the rules of the race. And although certain challenges were sometimes repeated, the outcome of the race was never the same.

The fair brought the people together, but the grandstand brought them alive.

Each demanding task was carried out in full view of the grandstand. When the contestant successfully completed the challenge, he had to crank his engine and race around the track for one or two laps. When he returned to the starting point, he shut off the engine and proceeded to his next formidable assignment. The race continued until all the challenges were finished.

Challenges ranged from something simple, like bobbing for apples or eating a blueberry pie with hands bound behind the back, to something a bit bizarre, like exchanging wardrobes. This meant the men had to change into women's clothes. Of course, the attire included ridiculous bits of under garments like a girdle that was usually too small, or a bra that was always over-sized. Picture a two-hundred-twenty-pound trucker jumping into an undersized pink girdle. Stretched to the very limit, it had to be especially painful for the man to race at high speed on a bumpy dirt track. To the spectators, it was riotous.

Orville Johnson ready to race in his Ford Model-T.

By far, the most hilarious challenge was the slippery pig. A speedy piglet covered in lubrication was almost impossible to catch or hold. The contestants were required to do both. To this day, I do not remember ever witnessing so many people becoming hysterical with laughter as when two slippery piglets eased through the wire fence into the audience in the grandstand.

In hot pursuit were two hefty Model-T drivers. The combination of a pair of Saint Bernard's on all fours in pursuit of two Olympic running piglets was literally bringing the grandstand down. Reserved chairs began to crash to the ground. Women screamed as their skirts took flight. Spectators rolled in the isles from laughter while some were physically brushed to the floor. If anyone was ever going to die from sheer laughter, that would have been the time.

In the big picture, what these people on the prairie shared in common brought them together. What made them

71

different brought strength to their steadfast character. And unlike many of the same small communities in the twenty-first century that have become warehouses of lost dreams and opportunities, theirs was a time of unlimited opportunity to fashion life in whatever way they imagined possible.

In a land characterized by a four-season climate, the warmth of summer brought a welcome reprieve from the wintry environment. Northern winter winds would hurl monstrous blizzards out of Canada. Stranded in white-outs, plains towns endured arctic temperatures of minus forty degrees Fahrenheit and below.

So when summer eventually announced its arrival on a warm southerly breeze, it was the answer to many prayers. We embraced that good fortune with America's favorite pastime—baseball. Who could forget the excitement as people crowded around the field to watch a championship baseball game played under the stars and bright lights of the city ball diamond?

We are not talking major leagues here, but rather neighborhood heroes who played, not for money, but for the pure love of the game. As self-made heroes of that period, they personified the "common man myth," with jobs to match. There was Tony the banker, Kenny the auto mechanic, Andy the teacher, and Sammy the farmer. Once in uniform, they rose to the status of gods that appeased the multitudes with their skill and dedication. One of my heroes, Tony Sipe, was inducted into the Minnesota Amateur Baseball Hall of Fame in 1986.

The game of baseball had always been an integral part of my community's early heritage. One of our most renowned baseball heroes was Walter Wilmot. He played on the 1881 team that won the Northwestern Amateur Championship by defeating Winnipeg, Grand Forks, Fargo, and Crookston. We were the

The baseball park as it looked back then and today.

Cinderella team of the nineteenth century that would go on to defeat every Goliath community they faced. As for Walter, he eventually went on to play professional ball with the Washington Senators in 1887 and the Chicago White Socks from 1890 to 1895.

Fortunately, even in the years of my youth several decades later, every youngster was admitted free, so I never had to miss a game. With a bit of luck and a pair of fast legs, I shagged enough foul balls to afford a bag of popcorn and a soda pop. Then I retired to the green wooden stadium behind home plate to cheer our heroes and boo the umpires. Today, the ball park still remains as one of the few memorabilia of that time period.

A closely-knit community did carry some disadvantages. For one, secrets were few and readily shared when discovered. Entire families for several generations were captured in the pages of an unwritten, but more often spoken, encyclopedia that covered the history of the community. Of course, confusion and discord were common because no one could ever be certain which version of history in current circulation actually contained the truth.

The most popular place to hear and expound on the collective knowledge of the community was within the confines of local food establishments. They displayed colorful names like Bluebird, Black Hawk, Silver Inn, and Green Lantern. Then there was the Red Star for those who favored a more liquid sustenance. One café managed to exist without color in its name. But it had a suggestive Freudian flavor nonetheless. Located at the junction of two major highways, truckers could fulfill their fantasies at the "Quickie."

As a young boy, no experience quite equaled the gathering of the locals at one of their favorite cafes. And that was especially true at the morning and afternoon coffee breaks. What made these meeting places unique besides the superb cuisine was the fellowship between ordinary men. Everyone understood that titles were left at the door.

Bonded together in an informal spirit, they unlocked the simple pleasures of everyday life by laughing at a good story or shaking dice in games like Horse or 6-5-4. The resounding hum of joyful voices, dice boxes pounding on counter tops, and the fragrance of freshly baked pastries carried an open invitation for everyone to crowd into the wooden booths or on wobbly stools lining the entire length of a long, narrow counter.

Surrounded by walls decorated with signs like Coca Cola, the kitchen flooded the air with the aroma of homemade pastry. By their uncanny ability to blend a simple combination of ingredients, each establishment carefully perfected their own tantalizing specialty. The result was that with each breath of air, everyone's stomach responded with hunger.

Come morning, the tantalizing scent of warm caramel and cinnamon-frosted rolls dominated the airways. In the afternoon, warm pies plumb full of apples or peaches or blueberries crowded the countertops. Other pastries, like German chocolate or a variety of frosted angel-food cakes, were cut and ready to be served up in generous proportions with whipped cream or ice cream.

What these frequent gatherings at cafés, and other places managed to accomplish was that they reinforced the community's bonding. That consensus of feeling would ultimately create an overall awareness of a distinct personal social permanence.

A social permanence that subscribed to the notion:
- A good day was a good day at work
- A good mother attended PTA meetings
- School discipline was corporal punishment, not suspension
- Gossip was an accepted medium for community news
- To be rich was to be alive and not have polio
- Coke with aspirin was considered an inappropriate intoxicant when mixed
- Sex education had not yet escaped the Dark Ages
- People could be happy and poor at the same time
- Church attendance invoked respectability
- Summer was the kind of heaven children aspired to
- Bunny hop, jitterbug, and butterfly were dances
- Cod liver oil was the miracle drug before penicillin
- "A penny saved was a penny earned" still had value
- Young Lutherans were not to dance because it was a sexually arousing sin
- Oatmeal and Cream of Wheat were the mothers' choice of champions for breakfast

No one ever makes the journey through life alone. Often the people we encounter during adolescence are destined to be more important than we can ever imagine. They have the capacity to influence our patterns of thought in unpredictable ways. In many respects, they become the shakers and movers who help identify and define what we were then, who we would become in the future—even what our children might be. For me, there were many who had exerted such an influence, but some were more memorable than others.

## Mom

When I began my journey through life, there had been an unexpected force that tried to take things away. But one thing that could never be taken from me was the confidence I derived from the good fortune of being raised by a mom with incredible devotion. I am not sure if she meant to give me that much confidence, as I sometimes felt myself to be invincible. In time, that invincibility would be put to the test over and over again. Peril-

My mom, Adeline Johnston.

ous adventures would push the very limits as I sought to cheat the devil to survive.

In the late 1800s, Mom's father, at the age of sixteen, abandoned the security of his family in his Norwegian homeland to sail alone to America. Fearless and adventurous like others of his time, he set his sights beyond the norm to a new land of opportunity.

Ironically, he ventured across an entire ocean and half a continent to settle in a small hamlet with the unlikely name of Climax, Minnesota. In this little prairie town near the place of my birth, he courted a young, pretty Norwegian. Dad later would poke fun at Grandpa's written announcement to his parents back home when he became betrothed to Grandma. Being a man of few words, Grandpa had written his parents the following brief announcement:

Dear Folks,

Found nice Norwegian girl in America. I intend to marry soon. We expect to live in Climax all our life. You betcha, I expect to be kept very busy. So I write again when I have more time.

Your loving son,
John

I would be remiss if I failed to mention that, in the same vicinity, there was another community named Fertile, Minnesota. When a local newspaper headlined a fatal automobile accident as: "FERTILE WOMAN DIES IN CLIMAX," the jokes never ceased. All things considered, I have always been grateful for the sensitive, fun-loving Norwegian heritage.

Mom, known by everyone as Addy, was the perfect role model for a woman living in the forties. She believed deeply in the accepted concept that her man was the absolute head of the household. To that end, she dedicated all her resources to make the only man she loved happy. It was a love defined in an immaculately clean home. Meals were catered to his preference. Dirty clothes were laundered and shirts ironed daily if necessary. Gardens were even planted with his favorite vegetables. Finally, in spite of long hours of work, she managed to remain attractive to the eye.

Years later, Mom never could come to grips with the woman's liberation movement. She'd ask, "What exactly do these women want to be free from?" For her, the generation that now demanded emancipation was too much for an early twentieth century mindset to understand.

When it came to the kitchen, Mom was a gifted cook like other moms of her time period. Located next to the kitchen sink was a drawer containing the most coveted books in the house, except for the Holy Bible—her Norwegian recipe books. Within those pages were ancient family formulas forged in the watery fjords of Norway by a generation of grandmothers. She also collected other legendary cookbooks that described an endless source of cuisines.

In fact, her coveted cookbooks had more influence on me than any book I ever read in early grade school. The one exception was the first grade reader book entitled *Dick, Jane and Spot*. But who could ever forget the emotional pride we felt in reading that first sentence, "See Spot run?"

Learning the poetry of food, the delicacies of past generations, became an obsession for me. It opened a window into the soul of those who endeavored to bring life meaning through taste and smell. To appreciate fully these gifted moms, one must first grasp a sense of the power and passion of what these dishes could bring to life. Keep in mind this was in a time when luxuries were few and far between. Television was not a common household item. Words like "stereo," "video," and "computer" were not in *Webster's Dictionary* or anywhere else.

What we did have were moms who flourished in their own world of baking. Nothing can transport my senses back to that time quicker than the aroma of fresh homemade bread or whole-wheat buns right from the oven. Tender with a light, tasty texture, they simply melted in the mouth like butter. But most memorable of all was my mom's pastries fashioned into supreme delicacies. They tempted and seduced even the timid to yearn for more than one helping.

I especially enjoyed a warm banana cream pie smothered in a lofty topping of sweet, fluffed egg whites rising in crests three inches above a most scrumptious homemade pudding. If cream pies failed to tempt one's passion, her chocolate chip pie was even more irresistible. It was a combination of melted marshmallows, thick whipped cream, and rich chocolate chips layered upon a bed of crushed graham crackers. After being cooled in the refrigerator, the pie delivered incredible bits of joy that lingered long after being consumed.

What made Mom's pies exceptionally unique was her simple Norwegian butter crust. Whether cradling strawberry, lemon meringue, blueberry, pecan, pumpkin, or peach filling, each pie was served up in a thin, tender crust that remained consistently firm yet delicate enough to crumble with the slightest bite.

If her variety of pies were not enough, she also offered cookies like molasses, sugar, oatmeal, raisin, date, and chocolate chip by the dozens. My favorite was a thin, crisp, buttery overnight cookie mixed with crushed walnuts. They simply melted as they touched your mouth. And they loved to be tenderly soaked in milk and consumed in large quantities.

By today's standards, Mom's repertoire of pies and cookies would, for most of us, be heavenly. But for Mom, it was only a beginning. She whipped up a buttermilk brownie with a freshly crafted chocolate fudge topping that would make even Betty Crocker take notice. At first taste, the response was inevitable, "Can I get the recipe?"

On special occasions, like Christmas, she orchestrated a cuisine of glorified rice smothered in whipping cream with small chunks of fresh pineapple and bananas, fruit cake sweetened by red cherries and cured in wrappings soaked in red wine. In addition, her Norwegian heritage was exalted in flat bread, *lefsa, krum kake*, and *lutefisk*.

Her superb desserts transformed adults into kids at a candy store eager to devour plates of Christmas cookies, home-made divinity, fudge, caramel corn, and apple strudel piled with freshly made ice cream. Fortunately, in those days, no one was aware of the ramifications of calories or cholesterol.

Once accustomed to her serene delicacies originating from the kitchen, I embarked at an early age to sharpen my own pastry skills. The learning experience became a valuable resource lasting a lifetime. Unfortunately, for Mom it became more of a nightmare.

Her kitchen, after one of my sessions as chef, looked like a battleground. Pools of flour coated the floor, as if a Minnesota blizzard had blown through. Door handles were slippery with grease. Sugar drifted into the cracks while spilled milk and juice created natural runoffs that painted the structural landscape of the kitchen floor into a variety of colors. By day's end, neither stove nor refrigerator nor window nor even ceiling remained unaffected by my efforts.

But in spite of every natural disaster, Mom continued to praise and extend her loving encouragement to me. She merely rolled up her sleeves and eradicated the mess with no feeling of regrets. Such commendable behavior can only exist in the realm of motherly love. Once I was married, I never again experienced that same harmonious tranquility in messing a kitchen.

Mom was accommodating in other respects as well. She always found time to be near my side when I was ill or sad. Clothes were cleaned and mended. Special requests from her kitchen were always honored. If any befitting term could characterize her loving and caring nature, it would be "generosity."

Over the years, there were times she would do without. Her willingness to give whatever she had without ever asking for anything in return was love in its most natural and purest form. It was a genuine love that could not be bought or taken, only given.

With meager wages as a beautician, she worked long hours on her feet. The texture of her hands was often raw and cracked from acid solutions. But in spite of all the hardships, she willingly endured the pain and sacrifice for her two boys to attend college. That unrelenting and unconditional love would one day build the bridge her children ultimately crossed over to build their own American Dream.

All across America, multitudes of other caring mothers, who were descendants of immigrants from far away places were expressing that same unselfish and loving dedication. They provided opportunities to their children that were not afforded to themselves. We were the first generation in a nation of ordinary families to go to college in large numbers. I would like to believe that our generation took that gift of love and sacrifice to excel and be everything they could be as a tribute. I know we did.

When Mom began school, she could only speak Norwegian. However, to her children, she had always spoken through her heart as she nudged us forward with the gentle strength of a loving spirit. Constantly present whenever we slipped from perfection, she was quick to make us feel loved and appreciated. Without her motivation and determination, our journey through life would have never been as successful.

# Dad

In contrast, Dad incorporated distinctly different characteristics, but his influence on who I would become was, nevertheless, equally important. Father's heritage evolved from a long line of self-made individuals. Their methods may have seemed crude by current standards, but they were the craftsmen of the time. No problem was ever too difficult to overcome. When Father needed a home for his new bride, he and Grandfather built one in their spare time. Complete with the basics of plumbing, electricity, and heating, construction was finished despite a severe lack of materials in a world at war.

I often wondered if Dad's German heritage influenced his need to exert control over his domain. Except for anger, Dad was never one to express his emotions. If he were troubled, no one could ever be certain except by his silence. He carried that ominous attribute to the very end. When faced with his own inevitable death, he remained in control by secretly choosing death on his own terms.

In life, he expressed himself best in his work. He personified

Dad's name was Percy Rodger Johnston.

82

perfection in every endeavor. Success was never expected to come without a lot of hard work and steadfast character. Of course, that same measure of excellence was expected of his young and untested apprentice. Dad's most memorable adage was, "Son, if you cannot do the work right, then it would be best that you did not do the work at all." These words immortalized the fundamental principal inherent in whatever he did. Eventually they evolved as a model for his young offspring. On the day of his funeral, I shared from the pulpit an incident underscoring that very principle.

The mortar between the bricks on his sister's chimney had weathered and come loose. According to Dad, someone had to remove and clean the bricks so they could be cemented once again into a structurally sound chimney. Even though I was a tad young, Dad was ready for me to begin learning everything he had learned from his father.

Age was never viewed as a barrier in making a man. Dad fully expected every individual to accept responsibility irrespective of age. According to his own father, the transition from boy to manhood was not just a process measured by time alone. It had to be forged through the experiences of one's own endeavors. This was a process that could not be transferred, but it had to be engineered individually.

Of course, his philosophical lesson was a bit over my head at the time. Still, the underlying message came across very clear. I was the chosen one to undo nature's destruction on top of a steep roof with no gutters to stop a fall. It was perfectly designed as a quick slide to eternity.

But, Dad was keenly aware that fear of heights was not a part of my resumé. He had already put me to that test by having me scramble through wooden rafters in the cattle barns. Then there was the grandstand, where I had to shimmy forty feet out onto a narrow, single two-by-six with one hand. The other hand was occupied with the insertion and removal of light bulbs for the fair. By comparison, his sister's roof looked like a walk in the park for me.

By noon of the next day, bricks had been removed and cleaned as instructed. Shortly after lunch, Dad arrived to provide additional instructions by demonstrating how to lay the first course of brick on the chimney base. He then departed knowing his standard of quality had been permanently laid in those bricks fashioned under my close scrutiny. By trial and error, it required the majority of the afternoon before my masonry skills slowly emerged. Well aware of dad's expectations, the wooden level left in my care was used with regularity to assure a straight and sturdy chimney.

As the sun was about to set, the familiar black pickup once again appeared at the curb. Climbing to the roof, Dad began inspecting the workmanship without a word spoken. After an intensive review of the chimney from one end to the

Auntie's house with the steep roof.

other he stood up straight, placed his hands on his hips and announced, "I see a problem."

He pointed to a single brick near the bottom just above the row he had laid. That brick had been awkwardly laid. As luck would have it, I had laid in an old worn brick with the smoother side facing outward. To prevent excessive accumulation of soot, a good chimney required that the smooth side of the brick always be placed on the inside. Most disturbing to me was the fact that only a keen eye could have ever spotted such an inconspicuous mistake.

In my defense, I quickly reminded Dad we were standing on a two level structure from which no one on the ground would ever notice such a trivial error. In addition, I pointed out that that particular brick faced the backyard, making its discovery even less likely. Saving the best argument for last, I expounded on the fact that, since the brick was so close to being smooth on both sides, who would care?

The reality of such an inconsequential mistake was to me as simple as my response. "If no one could discover the error, why bother to go though all the work to make the change?" Dad's eyes had remained focused on the chimney as he listened patiently. When I finished, he slowly turned around and paused for a moment. Looking down at me with fixed eyes, he replied in a voice deep in conviction and sincerity, "But I would know!"

My mind slipped into a blank. I was at a loss with no clear way to respond except with silence. The final verdict had been rendered. The next day every brick was unceremoniously removed and reassembled. The chimney lesson served as an enduring guide for a lifetime. Father avoided using a lot of unnecessary verbiage to explain what he wanted me to learn. Instead, he preferred that lessons be taught by example.

The fact that an error may never be discovered was not ever the important issue for him. What was important came down to the knowledge that I, his son, knew a wrong had been committed and found it acceptable. If the finished chimney was to be a reflection of myself, then, for Dad, a son who might settle for less than his potential was not acceptable. He knew who I would eventually become was dependent on those intrinsic values of integrity I set for myself from the very beginning. He was right. If any one lesson could be linked to my success in future endeavors, it had to be Dad's lesson on commitment to do the right thing without sacrificing one's own personal principles.

Although Dad never attained an education beyond the twelfth grade, he inherited an uncanny talent. He loved challenges. His life evolved and thrived by the measure of new ventures. With his imagination and tenacity to uncover solutions for any problem, he was proficient in the field of carpentry, plumbing, electrical, masonry, roofing, landscaping, and any other skill he desired to master. Remaining true to his nature, he subscribed to the same standard of excellence in each and every craft.

In the 1950s, his imaginative talent to learn the unlearned flourished into a new, successful appliance, television, and heating retail business. He never required any formal education or training. Instead, he mastered the technology of each of these new gadgets by taking them apart piece by piece. Then he would reassemble them taking specific notice as to what each component represented and how it functioned.

Endeavoring to be both an electrical contractor and a retail entrepreneur, he wasted no time in capturing his part of the American Dream. With the construction of a luxury home, attached garage included, life became easier for Mom. She no longer was required to harvest a garden for our winter food supply. We could even buy clothes with a designer insignia on the inside collar. As a family, we now ventured beyond the state line to destinations like Yellowstone Park.

By no means, did Dad's new enterprise make us wealthy. Filled with optimism and ambition, he seized the opportunity exemplified in the "common man myth." In doing so, he achieved for his family a better life then we had ever known. From his example, my brother and I would one day follow in his footsteps and uncover our own American Dream.

Graduating from the University of Minnesota and later completing a Masters Degree, my brother, Ron, advanced to the rank of colonel in the Air Force before retirement. He flew 110 combat missions in the Vietnam War and was decorated with the Distinguished Flying Cross. I graduated from law school with a Jurist Doctorate.

As parents, Mom and Dad could take pride in achieving an important milestone. As second-generation immigrant children, we had attained degrees that were seldom an option in their youth. Years later, the seeds of that earlier accomplishment sprouted even further. Three grandchildren achieved doctorate degrees in law, medicine, and psychology. Another received his MBA and one more finished her B.A. The fruits from their unrelenting efforts grew into a wonderful testament for future generations.

# John Henry

Our community had more than its share of interesting individuals with memorable attributes. Take for example the smart old codger who lived in a white house on the block adjacent to the Community Park with the band shell. We knew him by reputation, never by name, so we called him John Henry. What made John Henry memorable had more to do with the precious apple trees he treasured in his back yard. These were no ordinary apple trees. They produced a juicy, crisp apple found nowhere else, unless one was rich enough to purchase the bright-red, Delicious brand apples at the grocery store. For us, that was not an affordable option.

As an adversary, he turned out to be a rather formidable opponent to anyone desirous of his apples. Standing straight and tall with large ears and eyes deeply etched, he had an eccentric flair about him. We were certain John was a man without Christmas in his heart. Unwilling to share the wealth that hung on his trees, an inevitable skirmish line was arbitrarily drawn between him and us. The challenge would be measured in the resourcefulness and determination of youth pitted against a much older opponent embodied with the wisdom of age.

From the very beginning, John Henry had one distinct advantage. He knew he had the most desirable apples in town. And, although we knew it too, more important, he knew we knew. Tipping the balance of success in his favor, he ruled the apple orchard with a fist of iron in the form of a double-barreled shotgun specifically rigged with shells loaded with rock salt. The looming consequences of the gun upped the ante. It left no room for error. If the reward for victory was to be sweet, defeat would prove to be bitterly painful.

The stories of John Henry and his gun were legendary. Dad had often boasted how John seasoned more than one trespasser when he was a young boy. Even the staunch constable warned the public that John Henry was within his rights to use his salty lightning bolt to protect his precious assets from thieves.

In researching newspaper articles about my kidnapping, I learned that the law had been rather harsh to those caught stealing food. Chicken snatchers were sent to state reformatories for indeterminate sentences. They were not released until pardoned by the State Parole Board. That was a lot tougher than today's standards where I have seen losses of

$5,000 to even $75,000 not prosecuted by the feds. They claim it's all about priorities.

The force of law in John's case had its own priority. However, it would not be enough to deter hungry adventurers. Especially, those who had discovered that decision-making could be a lot more exciting when life and limb depended on it.

A few weeks prior to John's treasure becoming ripe enough for harvest I launched an intense effort to scout the layout of the property as well as spy on Mr. Henry's personal habits. The yard was rather small and simple. The stash of apple trees was clustered between a pair of white picket fences extending from the garage to the back porch. The only entry was through a locked gate next to the garage. John had carefully trimmed every apple tree high enough to allow clear visibility along the ground. As for the gun, it was concealed just inside the entrance from the back porch facing directly toward the apple trees.

By light of day and dark of night, I monitored John's sleeping habits, errands to town, church attendance, and any other peculiar trait that could create an opportunity. When the season of the apple arrived, diligent reconnaissance immediately reaped big dividends, but success was short lived. John soon became suspicious that his movements had been monitored. And although I was careful to remove only a few apples in a random manner so as not to call attention to their loss, John somehow knew they were missing. Like a good mother hen that carefully counted her chicks at the close of each day, he lived up to his vigilant reputation.

When the peak of the season approached, John began to skip church, stock up on groceries and sleep in random intervals. At night he left lights burning, making it impossible to determine if he was awake or asleep or if he was coming or going. In the dim light of an early evening, his silhouette could be seen with a long-barreled gun in hand. He looked like a pioneer waiting for marauding wolves.

As the apple war reached a higher level of intensity, I postured for a more tactical warfare by adding fresh recruits. There was no doubt that success to retain control over the prized apples would depend on how resourceful we could become. If we failed to be more imaginative, the initiative was lost.

Our first strategy was to decoy John by telephone. Fortunately, we had access to the phone of a classmate residing across the street. I volunteered to make the call. With my aunt as a switchboard operator I was familiar with how the system operated. The only drawback was to be certain Aunt Dot was not on duty. Recognizing my voice, she would definitely listen in to make sure I was not up to any shenanigans. She undoubtedly was more aware of my adventures than Mom with her direct access to the gossip hotline of the entire community.

Fortunately, when the operator asked, "Number please," I recognized the voice as belonging to someone other than my auntie. I quickly responded, "Number 27 please." After several rings, the sound of a deep, rough voice echoed from the other end of the line. I surmised it had to be John. Nevertheless, I politely asked, "Could I please speak with the owner?" When the voice growled that he was the owner, I waived an all-clear signal through the window with my cap. Those waiting for the sign began vaulting over the fence as I politely asked, "Could you please hold for my father who would like to speak with you?" While John remained patiently on the phone, the blitzkrieg attack launched upon his trees promptly surrendered a dozen or more fine apples to his enemy.

John was no dummy, however, so we took precautions never to repeat the same ploy. Our finest hour had to be the diversion we unleashed, so to speak, with the assistance of a stray dog. We purposely recruited a mongrel about the size of a full-grown bear to distract John. To accomplish that feat, the plan was to tie this monstrous dog securely to the entry latch on John's front screen door. By the time he untied the canine, we would have launched a quick raid from behind the garage. Victory was a calculated cinch.

By mid season, John had become leery of most anything suspicious. But we remained confident that this distraction could not be ignored. In the twilight of a quiet evening with a rib bone to pacify the stray dog, I tied a heavy-duty leash in a double knot to the handle of John's front screen door. After a series of hard raps, I quickly disappeared into the bushes.

When John appeared, he flashed on the front light and forcefully yanked the inner door open. His dramatic and unexpected appearance startled the dog so much that the mongrel exploded into the air. Launched from the steps, the dog managed with his sheer size to yank the entire screen door from it hinges. John was guarded by anger as he pursued his screen door bouncing down the street. I could not be sure if the panic-stricken dog was more afraid of the door or the large man just behind him, cursing at every step. Meanwhile, in the backyard, the assault on the trees proved to be a stunning victory.

By no means did every attempt end in a brilliant success. Some plans were too complicated and failed. Yet others were simple, but nevertheless succeeded—like the time we recruited a young neighbor girl to present an empty basket with a carefully written note inside. It read:

Dear John,
    We would be very grateful if you would kindly share a few apples with the family.
                        Thank you very much

It worked! Maybe John could not resist opening his heart to the charming innocence of a little girl. Then again, we could have been mistaken about John. Down deep he may have had a little charity in his heart after all. We would never know.

By season's end, we had vanquished our opponent with superior creative innovations without a casualty. I, for one, had no further desire to push our luck. However, Kit, a one-time adventurer, was insistent in making a final, quick raid. I made it quite clear from the beginning that I had no further interest in pursuing Henry's apples. Yet, he continued to beg and plead until I agreed to a very limited participation. The most I would do was knock on the front door to distract Henry's attention, but nothing more.

Kit had a reputation of being very quick on his feet. He had calculated any thirty-second diversion would be sufficient to grab a few apples and disappear. Not withstanding his speed, this hastily conceived plan had all the earmarks of a calamity in the making. For me, there was no risk in rapping on the front door. We had a lot of experience in the game of knocking on doors and disappearing. It was a common pastime when evenings became boring.

Just after sunset, we set about to approach John's yard from the white, wooden band shell in the city park. Apprehensive as to where John might be lurking, I decided to make my way to the front door by creeping close to the house foundation. The house had only one small light illuminating the parlor area. Reaching the front steps undetected, I extended one arm over the rail and rapped several loud bangs. Then I scurried to hide in a nearby bush.

When John jerked the door open he marched out onto the porch, glanced in both directions, quickly turned 180 degrees and marched back inside. From the very beginning, I knew John had not been fooled. He was probably racing back to the orchard. From the time his door slammed shut, I had counted to thirty when the silence of the evening was broken with the sound of two loud explosions.

My heart really began to thump. Cloaked in the darkness of the evening, I cautiously but quickly retreated. Moving low to the ground along the hedge lining the front sidewalk, I escaped to the corner of the property. Our designated rendezvous point was the band shell in the city park. To make certain no one had followed me, I circled the entire park and entered from the opposite direction.

From the soft sounds of moaning emanating from beneath the wooden platform, I gathered Kit had already taken sanctuary. Upon crawling into the small opening, I could see the faint outline of someone crouched on the dirt floor like a wounded animal. He was cuddling flesh wounds on both arms. The blood trickling down revealed several direct hits from pellets of rock salt. Fortunately, his long sleeved shirt absorbed much of the driving force exerted by the two blasts.

However, the agonizing pain of seasoned rock lodged firmly in Kit's raw flesh had unleashed a flood of tears down his cheeks. Uncertain of the seriousness of his wounds, I tried to respond calmly and knowledgeably. But the very thought of actually being shot with a double-barreled shotgun was hard to fathom. I had plenty of experience treating my own wounds from rocks, whips, and small B-B gun pellets. But these chunks of embedded rock salt represented an unknown challenge.

One alternative was to use the sharp point of my steel blade to force out the crusty rocks. But the inherent risk of that procedure was opening a larger wound or crumbling the bits into smaller granular pieces. I aborted that idea. Washing the wounds was not acceptable either because the water would only release the salt to create greater pain.

As I struggled to formulate a solution, Kit's agony was being expressed in a low, irregular whimper. It was clear that he was embracing the meaning of pain. He tried to appear upbeat when he said, "Doesn't hurt that much." But the tears that continued to dribble down both checks told a different story.

In the end, the only plausible answer was to resort to an unconventional alternative. Equipped with a natural pair of enameled incisors that could function like a portable tweezers, I began squeezing firmly down on each of the bleeding openings. Alternating between breathes of air I then exerted a vigorous sucking power like Mom's Hoover vacuum cleaner. Success could only be measured by the taste of course bits of salted fragments scratching the surface of my tongue. The surgical technique may have proved to be crude by medical standards, but within the dark regions of the band shell, we didn't care as long as it worked. And it did work. Sadly, Kit had dropped his armful of apples when shot. If he would have had ten seconds more, I believe the tragic result would have been averted.

John Henry had his final moment of victory with a little revenge. As for me, I was truly relieved that I had not been chosen to pay the price for John's brief taste of glory.

Fifty years later whenever I crunch a firm, juicy, crispy apple, I raise a toast to John's memory. He had challenged us to succeed despite the great risk. And like many adventures, he had spurred the imagination to be creative. I have often pondered one unanswered question. Was it mastering the challenge to capture the apple or was it the taste of the apple that was the real prize?

# Spooky

The adventures of John Henry will long be remembered for their formidable challenges. However, the experience with Spooky was entirely different. It began as a bizarre relationship that eventually transcended into a mythical encounter. Near the railroad tracks was a large, ominous house bare of paint and surrounded by thick lilac bushes. It was home to an extraordinary person whose very presence induced a sense of awe and mystery.

Neighbors had no memory of how long the house had existed. However, the trees surrounding the property were among the oldest and largest in town. Located near the tracks, the ancestry of the house could have been as early as the dawn of the railroad.

Every window was fully obscured with a gray and black substance. The condition was probably attributed to the inhabitant's extended use of kerosene for lighting rather than electricity. From the rooftop, the chimney bellowed a constant stream of smoke into the sky by night and day. In the yard, grass sprouted between thick patches of scrub vegetation extending in every direction. Overall, the landscape took on an eerie appearance more akin to the likes of the Shadow who crept into our homes through the airways every Saturday evening.

From within this intrusive landscape rose the legend of an incredible woman so strange in appearance, that her very presence provoked fear in young children. Living so close in proximity, I knew without any doubt I had to try to resolve the riddle of this mythical woman. Rumor suggested the best time to catch a glimpse of her was either at the crack of dawn or just after sunset. During those brief intervals when it was neither day nor night, she often wandered about the property in the twilight.

Early one morning before the light of day, I secretly crawled through the dark shadows to hide within a thick lilac bush lying between the house and woodshed. As birds greeted the morning sunrise with their melodies, the back door creaked open. Slowly a conspicuous silhouette emerged. As it proceeded from the long shadows of the porch I was introduced to a figure of horror movie proportions.

Standing upright like a solid fifty-gallon drum, the creature was draped in white cloth hanging straight down from two oversized shoulders. Perched upon the crown of its head was a noticeable large, round bald area. It was shiny as though recently varnished. Encircling this polished skin, I could see strands of snow-white hair drooping in irregular lengths.

As she stepped from the shadow of the porch, I surmised this abnormality had to be the mystery woman. Captured in an incredible physique, she boldly waddled like a large, indomitable turtle swaying from side to side. Spying from ground level beneath the bush, I focused on her large, round frame balanced precariously on a pair of stocky, bowed legs. It was an incredible sight.

Unexpectedly, her methodical journey to the woodshed suddenly halted. With a pair of small, black-marble eyes sunk deep within her face she scanned the landscape like a submarine periscope. I immediately froze and held my breath. Detecting nothing out of the ordinary, the swaying motion continued to the woodshed only a few yards from where I lay motionless. Then, for the second time, without any warning she swirled to stare directly in my direction. It was as though some inborn instinct had relayed a message that danger was near.

I had every expectation that she might have the power to hear the ground breathing beneath me. Just in case, I began holding my breath once more. In addition, I took the precaution to cover a hand over my heart. It was at this point I noticed a large flap of skin extending from her chin down to her chest. As her head continued to twist from side to side, the exaggerated flap of skin quivered like Jell-O shaken in a bowl.

For the first time, I slowly began to grasp the reality that my eyes were staring into a strange, indescribable world. With eyeballs about to bulge from their sockets, the flapping movement of her chin produced a hypnotic effect. When she finally turned away to enter the woodshed, I quietly slipped away. On the way home, I pondered whether it was possible to be snared under the spell of this most unexplainable creature.

Years later I would discover the abnormal skin under her chin was only a goiter. The condition was not mysterious, merely an enlargement of her thyroid gland. It was apparently common in the populace of that time period. However, during the superstitious age of my early childhood, the possibilities of what or where this unusual creature had originated were endless. I began to envision Spooky as a kind of super being capable of most anything.

She had stirred my imagination with many questions. Could it be possible that her origin was from some mysterious place? And if she had the power to cast a spell, would I be strong enough to resist? To discover the many unanswered questions about this legendary figure was as compelling to me as any other adventure.

One conclusion was certain. Her secretive existence compelled a return to search for an answer. Admittedly, finding other fearless volunteers to pursue a quest into a haunting domain was not easy. By now, the infamous woman had been bestowed with the name "Spooky." Her unforgettable, scary image befitted the nickname.

One afternoon as we headed off to the river by way of the railroad, we unexpectedly spotted Spooky. She was standing alone in broad daylight near the front sidewalk in her long, white gown. This was a rare occasion. The temptation to maneuver a quiet and undetected approach from her hind side was overwhelming.

As soon as we had crept close enough to almost reach out and touch her ghostly image, she suddenly turned and glared down at us. We instantly froze, and our mouths dropped wide open without a sound. In response, she rolled her round eyes straight up into her forehead causing the pupils to completely disappear. With only the whites of her eyes showing, she blared out a high-pitch, wordless scream. Simultaneously my friends and I, shocked by this, jumped high into the air and raced off like a gang of roadrunners.

Haunted by her eerie image, we were convinced something was very supernatural about Spooky. The decision was made to risk one final attempt to discover the true origins of this strange neighbor. We were certain the answer was hidden somewhere in her old, haunted house. However, no one seemed to be brave or dumb enough to slip into her castle for a look, except for me.

The prospect of being captured within the confines of Spooky's eerie abode had me thinking that just maybe some things did not need an explanation. But I was not willing to surrender my curiosity. At the same time, I was under no illusion that I could breach her fortress without repercussions. Eventually, a compromise was reached. We would return under the cover of darkness to observe activities through the looking glass of the window. If the old windows covered with soot prevented clear visibility, I would enter through the back door. The others would create a diversion around the front porch. (We had learned a lot having dealt with John and his apples.)

When the evening of our journey to enlightenment arrived, only two others had enough courage to seek out the truth. It was a perfect night for our mission—just enough clouds blanketed the moon to obscure any chance of being discovered too easily. Slithering through the grass near the rear of the house, we headed towards the faint light in the window half way to the front porch.

Quietly tucked out of sight in the flower bed beneath the dim light, we peered over the wooden ledge. Faces tightly pressed to the smoke-stained glass, we saw very little, but the place almost seemed abandoned. Then we spotted the silhouette of a body lying motionless on the floor. Lit by candles, the large, square room flickered with a light that caused shadows to dance on the wall and ceiling. But all eyes remained fixed on that figure stretched like a corpse in the middle of the floor. What worried us was that the motionless body was obviously too small to be that of Spooky.

The dim light had revealed other secrets. On the far side of the body, we could see pieces of furniture darkened as though soiled by years of human use. The wallpaper was shadowed with stains much like the windowpane. For the next five minutes, everything remained quiet on both sides of the glass. From time to time, I would catch myself unintentionally holding my breath as I listened to the sounds of night crickets chirping and mosquitoes buzzing.

By now many more questions than answers were popping in and out of my consciousness. Was the body a relative of Spooky? Was it alive? Did the candles have some strange, ritual meaning? Would we discover that beyond the long, dark shadows, other abominable creatures lurked around the corner? Were we about to witness the horrors of what others had shrugged off as Halloween delusions?

Every unanswered question brought a new rush of excitement. At any moment, I fully expected some movement or interaction would bring the intense curiosity to a thrilling climax. The balance of risk and reward weighed heavily on my mind as attention concentrated on the inside of the house. So much so, that I lost every bit of awareness of our immediate surroundings.

Unexpectedly, a strong grasp took hold of my shoulder. Petrified, I turned. Towering over me like some graveyard ghoul draped in her gown was Spooky. Weak-kneed and momentarily subdued by her intense grip, my entire sensory system zoomed into deep space. It became one of those moments when one is compelled to make a life-or-death decision.

Too young to become a ghostly victim, I bolted straight into the air and raced off into the dark. The others were not far behind. As we cleared the neighbor's hedge, we heard the familiar high-pitched screeching call. I knew it could only be Spooky sending a final warning to never return. I could live with that. At the moment, my only concern was to get as far away as possible.

Because our contact with Spooky had been such an eccentric encounter, it was a benchmark to an important awakening. I had seen some weird characters pictured in comics and in the explorations in space with Flash Gordon on television. But I had never given any thought that actual people could be so strange. And although I was wrong about Spooky from that point on, in many respects, she had stirred within me a curiosity. She had touched our imaginations. I would never again view people in quite the same, innocent way.

# Ramus

I believe children remain remarkably the same generation to generation. For example, consider my young neighbor Ramus. As a kid, Ramus was clean-cut, mild-mannered and had no particular distinguishing characteristic except for his uncanny ability to consume dirt. Whenever we baked gumbo mud cookies and dried them on the hot sidewalk, we invited

Ramus to taste them. What made his feat eerie was the unassuming manner in which he consumed a cookie of dirt. His face would brighten up with heavenly joy as he refused to surrender himself to the knowledge he was actually eating dirt.

His mannerism was like a kid feasting upon candy from the rows of jars at the Five & Dime on Main-Street. In fact he was so convincing, it almost tempted me to try one for myself. But I never did. Years later, my wife, Lynn, shared a similar experience with a playmate in her neighborhood. The young girl also consumed cookies baked of dirt as though they were bites of joy.

Later in life, I often wondered if the reason behind this bizarre appetite had more to do with a lonely childhood. Maybe Ramus had no one to share a kind moment with. In the absence of friends, even the rude mockery of other children may have been acceptable if it provided needed attention.

If true, I should like to meet Ramus again someday. I would shake his hand and say that I was sorry. We were just too young to understand. I would share with him how our experience together provided a framework from which our children were taught at an early age to view others by their heart and not by appearance or different mannerisms.

# Sher

There is an old cliché: "We are known by the company we keep." If true, Mom must have had her share of doubts as to what bizarre direction her youngest offspring was heading. In the first place, I exerted more effort to be among the birds and earthly creatures of the woodland than with my family. Second, for a brief period, I spent the duration of my available time with the girl who lived across the street.

Like "two peas in a pod," we shadowed each other as though inseparable. Her real name was Sharon, but I called her Sher. For an entire summer, we rode bikes, shared numerous adventures, ate meals together, slept overnight at each other's homes, camped out, built forts, played games, peddled lemonade on the curbside and organized circus events in my dad's garage. I even consented to wearing one of her dresses in a circus act. We shared what appeared to be a never-ending relationship bonded together by an implicit trust that only our hearts could understand.

I no longer remember every distinct feature about Sher. What I do remember is that she always had a soft glow about her. With brown hair and brown eyes that smiled, her natural permanent tan was a pretty match. She was born a gifted listener who would silently communicate with a warm smile I always could understand.

Together with Sher in one of her dresses and Dean prior to a circus performance.

But perhaps the most redeeming virtue we shared was a yearning for adventure. Often barefooted like myself, ready to follow anywhere, brave in the dark of night, fearless of crawling, wiggly creatures and unfettered by gender differences, we linked together in ways others could never imagine, and adults never understood.

In the morning, there were times I sensed she was waiting for me to find her to begin another day. It was a silent communication not in words but from one mind to the other.

This divine feeling of innocence absent of any adulterant comes only once in a lifetime. It is a phenomenon reserved for the very young, Only in that privileged world of the untested and untroubled does it reign supreme. This is a world where the pure, unrestrained spirit is free to explore and share without the restraints of adulthood. Hopefully, children will always have that rare opportunity to experience their own kindred spirit free from obscurity, yet pure in thought.

My timeless summer with Sher has remained one of the fondest and most memorable periods of early childhood. It was a time when the magical forces of our innocence converged to become an immaculate bond.

Sometimes our most memorable experiences can also become our most inspirational. My fanciful vision of that summer with Sher was later translated into a compelling inspiration as a teenager. I wanted to transcribe a series of poetic rhythms in the quest to discover love. Remembering how it was in the beginning, I began my writings with a prayer.

## A Prayer to an Unknown Love

Our Father in heaven above,
Help me find the one I love.
Little do I know of this love in my dream.
Her essence is no more real than an angel might seem.
Help me to know her with a touch true and pure.
Make her presence ever longing to be near.
And when the time comes, bind us in a love forever
That will share the joy in living eternally together.

Amen

# Grannie

If I could have written her epitaph, the inscription on Grannie's stone would have recited:

Born to German parents, September 8, 1891, Lucia E. Johnston had always taken comfort in knowing that life had been good to her. Self-reliant, strong, proud and seemingly invincible, she stood straight and tall whenever faced with adversity. She avoided foul language, alcohol and tobacco and never allowed age or any individual to alter her will or the style in which she elected to live. Children were delivered at home, and she never experienced the inside of a hospital for the first ninety years of her life. Death had come prematurely at 104 for Lucia suffered from no illness, only idleness.

Everyone in the community, whether they were family or neighbors, called Lucia "Grannie." What captured their imagination was her embodiment of the doctrine of Americanism. Like other first-generation Americans, she had separated herself from other countrymen and family still living in the homeland. Free to express a newborn spirit, she flourished in a life that personified her own distinctive characteristics.

When her husband, William, perished in the Red River flood of 1947, Grannie vowed on his deathbed that there would never be another man in her life. She never broke that promise. During those last fifty years, I was fortunate to share her legacy. Now I want to share it with you and the generations yet to be born.

It is impossible to capture all the emotion and perception someone like Grannie can bring to life. Graced with an easy, un-

pretentious manner, she pursued her journey through life with an endless source of energy from the break of dawn to the fading sun.

The bountiful gardens she planted sustained her for an entire year. Chickens raised from hatchlings grew to become prize canners by fall. Fiercely self-determined, she boiled up her own soap, sewed beautiful quilts for every family member, chopped firewood for the winter, mowed grass by hand, raked leaves for mulch to enrich a much-coveted strawberry patch and raspberry thicket, canned an entire food cellar, ground feed by hand to feed the chickens, attended church regularly, and cooked nutritious, tasty delights. My particular favorite was her special vegetable soup with fresh garden vegetables and chunks of roast beef. I also savored the ginger-man cookies covered in fluffy white frosting.

Her free spirit, warm expressions, and love for life became an inspiration for a lifetime.

Life with Grannie was never boring. With a property right on Main Street, her backyard transformed an ordinary city life into a thriving natural habitat. Towering oak trees climbed high into the sky to provide a home to squirrels and nesting robins. Lilac bushes that boasted blooms of purple and the thick hedges bordering the property sheltered nests for a variety of young hatchlings.

Directly behind the house, hens cradled fresh, warm eggs in nests of straw. The open-fenced courtyard attached to the hen house was reserved for

The grandfather I would never have the chance to know.

the old hens and their cocky overseers. It was normally a place to feed, water and exercise. But for some, like the roosters, it was an arena to establish their pecking order by combat if necessary.

Come fall, Grannie could be seen in that same courtyard with one leg resting on top of a large, round, chopping block. With an ax in one hand and a chicken clutched by both feet in the other hand, she wielded that iron ax like some warrior Viking. The carnage did not stop until every chicken placed under the sentence of death had its head delivered to the guillotine.

With so many heads rolling to the ground, headless bodies were taking flight everywhere at once. Air traffic became so dangerously congested that decapitated chickens collided in mid-air. When they came crashing to the ground, one could hear an eerie sound emitted from a squawk box deep within.

When the slaughter was finished, Grannie would reward her helpers with fresh, pan-fried chicken livers. Rolled in flour and salt and crystallized to perfection in a hot, iron skillet with a complement of sautéed onions, the crispy tidbits melted in your mouth.

Grannie's ancestry must have been agrarian. Located beyond the chicken enclosures were the first of two major gardens. The garden parallel to the street was reserved for row plants like carrots, radishes, onions, corn, and beans. The garden between the small barn and the chickens contained vine plants such as squash, cucumbers, muskmelon, watermelon, and tomatoes. If manna spilled from any chosen vine within her Garden of Eden, it had to have been from her tomato plants.

Each year she selected the seeds from the finest and best-tasting tomatoes. Over the winter, these hybrids were tenderly nurtured for next year's crop. How she captured the essence of life lying deep within a choice tomato was in many ways a measure of how she pursued her own life. She always looked for the best and managed to discover it.

As for Grannie's home, it was fashioned in the tradition that people relished a special relationship with the front porch. While porches of today are built to behold spectacular views of water, valleys, or mountains, her porch had the distinction of looking directly onto Main Street. In fact, the sidewalk virtually abutted the entire length of the structure. Fortunately, her squatter rights entitled from the horse- and-buggy days preempted any issue of legal setback or right-of-way. However, her free-roaming chickens did not inherit that same legal privilege. When townfolks wanted to exalt Main Street into a modern retail center, the signs were clearly against Grannie.

Chickens had always formed an essential part of her existence. Whether baked, fried or canned, they were as important a commodity to her life style as rice to the Chinese, or tea to the English, or wine to an Italian. She was quick to point out that her chickens had been a part of the town's landscape long before these would-be chicken abolitionists had shed their diapers.

Moreover, these were not just ordinary, dumb, country chickens. And she was right. Stories of her cunning city chickens had become legendary. Rumors suggested that her feathered family members were in some ways guided by their own intellect.

For over thirty fowl generations, Grannie routinely released the entire flock of chickens each morning. Under the careful leadership of high-ranking roosters, the entire flock navigated safely across Main Street unattended by human assistance. Once across, these same roosters skillfully guided

Grannie on her porch during a time when the horse was as popular as the automobile.

their followers to the railroad tracks to feast on grain spilled from the loading and unloading of rail cars adjacent to several elevators.

Come late afternoon, the roosters gathered up the hens for the dangerous journey home. The procedure was not much different from sheepdogs rounding up their flock of grazing sheep. However, these roosters also displayed the uncanny ability to keep their own time. Whether it was by position of the sun or some internal clock, even workers at the elevators knew when the workday was drawing to a close by using "rooster time."

The journey back home was closely regimented. Marching their hens away from the tracks, the roosters directed the flock in a tight circle with no stragglers. Reaching Main Street, the exalted leadership halted and huddled their feathery wards close together. Then the top-ranking roosters would boldly step forward onto the passageway. Stretching and twisting their necks upward and sideways, they appeared to be looking and listening in both directions to determine when it was safe to cross. Grannie always bragged how her roosters had never lost a hen to a train, a horse or, in time, a motor vehicle.

Roosters that exhibited this unusual trait of rational thought were handsomely rewarded in the fall by keeping their heads. Who knows, just maybe some of those shrewd roosters that managed to avoid the ax did pass on some of their genetically acquired behavior. Perhaps that's what Grannie intended.

I was somewhat dubious on that subject until I listened to a special news story on CNN in 2002. A recent study had confirmed that chickens had a much higher intellect than previously known. In fact, they were now ranked higher than the pig. This was a significant discovery because a pig, like a dog, was trainable. If Grannie had been alive to hear the CNN report, she would have grinned before her skeptics and said, "I told you so."

But back in the early fifties, Main Street was being measured in terms of progress. Retail merchants soon banded together to restrain Grannie's chickens from having the run of Main Street. It was only a matter of time before their complaints compelled serious consideration by the city fathers. Exercising the right of eminent domain over the chickens, they eventually adopted an ordinance prohibiting any fowl to be loose within city limits.

All things considered, the ordinance was reasonable. Grannie still retained her chickens on Main Street but was prohibited from allowing them to spread their foul presence beyond the property. I like to believe the city fathers were very understanding and sympathetic to a widow whose husband had served the community in many roles. After all, they could have enforced an ordinance prohibiting her chickens altogether.

In the end, the city had allowed Grannie to retain her precious style of living. As for the community, a portion of their own cultural heritage had also been preserved. The roosters expressed their own gratitude as they marked the beginning of every morning and evening by crowing their hearts out for everyone on Main-Street. If there was an irony in this chicken legend, it might be in one simple statement. The city had succeeded in removing the fowl from Main Street, but they could not succeed in removing Main Street from the fowl.

Overnights with Grannie provided a perfect opportunity to escape the confines of parental care. Without the advantage of unrestricted freedom, many of my mischievous adventures would not have been possible. Halloween was one of those special occasions. When evening descended, the carved pumpkins were lit, and a flurry of activity erupted in the shadows from tipping outhouses by the ballpark to soaping messages on windowpanes. For most of the younger children, the phrase "trick or treat" meant a bag full of sweet treats. On the other hand, for some, the real treat was delivering a bag of tricks.

More often than not, a kid who had never considered doing anything wrong would find himself caught up in the frenzy of an irresponsible prank. Recognizing potential trouble, law enforcement always took the precaution to swear in extra deputies. Volunteer firemen remained near the station ready for the unexpected. With the number of tricksters they suspected were on hand, they probably knew there was no way mischief could be avoided. It was safe to assume that most of them probably participated in their own devilish deeds when younger. Tensions remained high. Someone was bound to shoot for the "big one," something that would excite the multitudes.

Outhouses had become a favorite target on H-Day. But to launch a full-scale assault to up end an entrenched outhouse took a certain degree of muscle power. At least they were more than I could muster, but not for my brother Ron and two other boys with the same name. One might have been our next door neighbor, Vilmo.

Having dumped the outhouses by the ballpark on previous occasions, these three Musketeer conspirators had perfected their expertise. The logistics were simple. They would wait until the cover of darkness, sneak along the ditched creek behind the homesteads, avoid the outhouses that were closely guarded and attack a vulnerable target with the greatest of speed. Every detail of their operation had worked to perfection, except when the proprietor of one particular outhouse moved his structure forward to accommodate his unwelcomed guests.

Apparently, this owner had stored the memory of strategies of previous years. Racing through the dark to tip the outhouse, the tricksters plunged into an open pit full of you know what. It would be difficult to imagine being buried in anything worse.

The Halloween I remember most began when a group of older country boys decided to highjack two wagons loaded with straw. They were bound and determined to build a barricade across West Main Street adjacent to the creamery plant.

Grannie and her friends, tucked into the porch at the end of the block, watched as kids migrated in from all over the city as the news of the prank traveled. From the very beginning, the sheer numbers and the mood of those gathered set the stage for a lot of excitement and attention. Too young to be physically involved, I worked my way just close enough to feel the pulsating energy of the hyperactive teenage crowd.

Like a well-coordinated hive of bustling hornets, the youths barricaded the street in no time. The audacity to undertake such a project in open defiance of the constable was awe-inspiring. But what happen next was even more memorable.

Two older teens stepped out from the crowd. One was a slender, muscular boy decked out in a black leather jacket. His dark, duck-tailed hair was a perfect match. The other teen was a slender, fully developed, red-haired girl. She was draped in a long, white-sleeved shirt. Both sleeves were one quarter rolled back and the collar was raised around her neck. This was the fashion of the time.

The two were picture-perfect teen idols. Theirs was a match made in heaven, except for one problem. Their gods reigned in separate and distinctly different heavens. The boy's family was Catholic. She was Lutheran. But on that night they would defy the prejudice that had kept them apart. They wanted to make a statement in front of everyone and to themselves. As the two proceeded to climb to the top of the barricade, the crowd understood and began chanting, "Go, Go, Go."

Once on top, they joined hands and raised them high into the air in a defiant gesture that inspired allegiance. I had experienced that similar charisma only once before. It was in the movie, *The Wild and Reckless*. The untamed and explosive young Marlon Brando had expressed a similar sentiment in his studded, black-leather jacket.

If I remember correctly, that scene was right before the trouble began. Knowing what little I did about the local constable, I kept thinking how pissed off he was going to be when he arrived on this disorderly scene. And the question was never *if*, only *when*.

Judging from the number of kids constantly looking over their shoulder, I suspected many must have shared the same sentiment. Maybe for that very reason, someone opted to torch the barricade. Suddenly, flames were spurting high into the dark, creating a shower of floating sparks.

The whole scene was reminiscent of the bonfire prior to the annual football homecoming game. As everyone began chanting the high school Viking cheers, the town's fire whistle sounded. Then the scream of sirens signaled it was time to retreat. Those who had gathered for the celebration scattered in very direction. For Grannie and her friends, it must have been a great show. As for me, I knew Dad would be with the fire truck, so I quietly slipped away into the dark alley.

I recognized the older boy on top of the haystack. His family lived on a farm. In appearance and personal charisma, he had it all. Many years later, the picture of him and the girl standing hand in hand together flashed into my memory when I watched *West Side Story*. I often wondered if the two of them had a better ending than the movie.

Waking the next morning at Grannie's was a different kind of adventure. It began with the music of wood crackling from the belly of the old iron cookstove. Shortly the rhythmic beats of lard spitting and popping signaled that the large iron skillet was ready. The alarm to rise came when the aroma of eggs and bacon began to permeate the air. It was followed by the scent of freshly baked biscuits that beckoned company.

After a robust breakfast, I was ready for chores. Together with my trusty Ranger Red Ryder, I patrolled the chicken enclosure to prevent the masked, bandit sparrows from stealing the chicken feed. I was also entrusted to hunt down the mousy intruders claiming homestead rights to the hen house. But the most time-consuming chore was cutting the lawn with a push mower. However, once evening arrived, all work was set aside whether finished or in progress.

Grannie and friends paid strict adherence to a long-standing American custom of gathering on the front porch every evening. Perched high in lofty advantage adjacent to the sidewalk on Main Street, her screened gallery was virtually unnoticeable. It provided uninterrupted eavesdropping to the end of the block. And of course, every conversation became fair game.

Quietly concealed in the dark shadows, Grannie and friends patiently sat for hours. Like black widow spiders, they eagerly waited to pounce on any secret or gossip shared by unsuspecting strollers on the sidewalk. For the viewer, it was like a front-row seat to their very own live performance of a soap opera like, *As the World Turns*. They claimed to have overheard more gossip than her daughter at the phone company. Well, almost as much. Over the years, her porch became so popular that she had to take precautions to avoid overbooking.

Occasionally, I provided additional entertainment by, from the top of the house, tossing rotten tomatoes or large, ripe cucumbers down on unsuspecting motorists cruising Main Street. Whenever one of those large, mushy cucumbers struck the soft hood of a vehicle, a loud *ka-bang* broke the silence of the evening. Inevitably, after each loud boom, a low giggle

Grannie's enclosed porch with removable windows provided easy access to conversations as pedestrians strolled by.

arose from within the porch. Surprisingly, during all those years, Grannie never scolded me nor shared any of my prank-ish deeds with Dad or Mom.

I guess my mischievous ideas had served as a reminder of her son, who was my dad. She shared a few of the pranks he used do pull, like hot-wiring the living room couch to transmit an electric impulse that greeted house guests with a "bottoms up" shocking welcome. Until that little bit of history was known, I had never pictured Dad as a child. And when my own son was growing up, I discovered he had inherited that same mischievous behavior.

As the family matriarch, Grannie sought neither fame nor fortune but found both. Living in a wealth of time to the age of 104, she was crowned the oldest living resident in Norman County. On her 100th birthday, she pulled me aside and asked, "Do you have any idea why God has kept me alive so long?" She figured he might have wanted her to start life over again. My immediate response was that she had envisioned the perfect answer. I replied, "Next year we will celebrate the first year of your new life."

Grannie playing cards at the age of 104.

Grannie passed from our lives four years later while playing a hand of rummy with friends. When the flood waters reappeared in the spring and covered her grave site next to Grandpa, I could not help but wonder if maybe God had more than one reason for her longevity. At the funeral, my favorite cousin, Sondra, who was more like a sister, wanted to know how I would manage without Grannie. With watery eyes, she said, "Grannie's departure has created a sorrowful void in my life."

Sadden by her expression of grief, I replied that for me Grannie could never die. The memory of her free spirit, her warm expressions, her loving essence for life, and her strength to persevere brought an inspiration that would flow strong within my veins forever.

From the very beginning, I had loved Grannie as fiercely as anyone could ever love a mom. Yet, I always knew it would be a silent love. But in that unspoken world, she has remained the most beloved grandmother and secretive mentor in my life.

# Preacher

As a youngster, any impression I had of religion was not much different than that of school. Both institutions were mandatory and each pursued strict standards of discipline. One was in the form of a stern look, the other with a swat of a yardstick or the jerk of an ear. Prayers, like lectures in the classroom, often dawned on the brink of eternity. And in place of a teacher, we had a preacher guided by the Holy Book instead of the *Daily Reader*.

Both had high expectations of sacrifice as a prerequisite to success, and they carried a price for failure. In addition, each sovereign demanded dues paid immediately for a reward we could expect in some distant future neither could predict.

Consequently, religion imagery proved too regimented and its doctrine too demanding. God was much easier to commune with when surrounded in a natural cathedral of his own creation. In that setting, one could always sense a connection to something bigger than oneself. And this still works for me today.

In spite of the mandatory rituals of attending Sunday school, church, weekly school release classes, Christmas/ Easter programs, Methodist Youth Fellowship (MYF), summer bible school, and church camp, no experience quite equaled the annual revival meetings.

Every summer, at the peak of hottest days in August, the Holy Ghost summoned the faithful. The fairground property was reborn from the pagan days of the carnival and christened the chosen land. Upon that hallowed ground was constructed a divine tabernacle beneath a looming canvas tent. Within its sanctuary stood the pulpit perched on a high stage erected to the rear. Rows of wooden planking for seating extended from the stage to the rear exit.

This canvas temple was home to a master of the English language. He could verbally abuse the devil himself and still walk away triumphantly. As the dominant player, his appearance was easily distinguishable from everyone else's. He stood erect in a dark suit with a white shirt and tie neatly knotted. With hair carefully combed in shiny grease, he marched arm in arm with the authority of God Almighty. His sermons had the divine power to deliver up any soul lost somewhere between Heaven and Hell.

With a direct line to God, he carried a booming voice that would cry out into the darkness of evil. His mannerisms created an atmosphere of intense feeling and general excitement. No one could be certain if at any given moment the Kingdom of Heaven might descend upon the earth under that very tent. And when he prayed for someone to recover from a serious infliction, and that recovery occurred, it was an answer to his prayers. And if they died, it was "God's will."

The finale of the evening was always the highlight of the program. And the script never changed year after year. When the piano began playing softly in the background, the preacher whispered into the microphone lyrics from old religious favorites carrying the message, "Softly and tenderly Jesus is calling for you and for me, 'Come Home, Come Home.'" As the tempo of the music turned upbeat, the volume increased. It was the signal for the spiritually weak and

weary seeking salvation to begin trudging forward to the platform.

At that same time, I was being very cautious never to
turn my back to the stage. These roving preachers could never
be trusted to remain on the platform. As "Soul Collectors," if
the catch of the day were not large enough, they would begin
roaming among the crowd. At about that time, I was asking
Mom, "Can we go now?" Carefully plotting an emergency exit
in the event one of them attempted to lay his hand upon me,
Mom would reply, "No and quit wiggling around."

Unfortunately, formal religion left more of an impression of ambiguity on me than any sense of comfort.
Consequently, I managed to steer a wide birth of all preachers
in my early youth. However, not all journeys in life are ours
alone to determine. As fate would have it, the boy unexpectedly came face to face to challenge one of the Lord's servants on
the plains of the prairie. This would be a day neither preacher
nor boy would ever forget.

Railroad beds and city streets on our side of town had
one noticeable link. Both contained an abundance of the hard
mineral substance most people referred to as rocks. In my
world, they were bullets for the slingshot or hand grenades to
be tossed. I cannot remember any boy who could resist the
temptation to pick up a rock and give it a throw. But like certain sins, some boys were tempted more often than others.

Everyone old enough to distinguish one home from
another could have enlightened a person that the white house
with the big porch in the block adjacent to the tracks was a parsonage. The church was situated on the corner leading to Main
Street. However, I was not old enough to make such distinc-
tions.

On this particular summer day, life began on an upbeat.
By noon, I had raced up and down the country ditches and
found three empty pop bottles. I returned them to the Black

Hawk Café near the tracks for my reward. There was a two-cent refund for each bottle. I immediately invested five cents in a pack of sunflower seeds and splurged a penny for one wrapped piece of bubble gum. I actually preferred the two-cent box of snaps, but they were too easy to consume. And, with the expectations of a big day in the country, one had to be equipped with a long-lasting treat as a companion.

Following those same tracks to the river, an unexpected rock fight erupted. Why? Sometimes why was never important. What did prove to be important was that it would be three against one. In spite of the odds, experience in handling rocks, tipped the fight in my favor. Anyone with the courage to take a few hits had an added advantage. In no time, all three opponents bolted and made a hasty retreat. As they raced off to seek refuge in the white house with the big porch across the street, I cocked my arm and let fly a barrage of heavy missiles.

Now anyone who has thrown rocks understands flying rocks play no favorites. Furthermore, when they strike, they can cause havoc and pain indiscriminately. As my guided projectiles approached their intended target, the only girl of the three glanced back and was sadly struck on the side of her face.

Upon impact, a loud, blood-curdling scream was released that vibrated through the entire neighborhood. From out of nowhere, a man dressed in a dark suit with a white shirt charged up the block from the church. He picked up the injured girl and cradled her in his arms on the wooden porch. There was little doubt in my mind that he was more than a little concerned about the fallen girl.

My heart told me to stay, but every other instinct was sending an urgent message to run. As I hesitated, the man in black, with a white shirt and tie, brought back memory flashes of a preacher man of some sort. When the injured girl was helped inside with the assistance of a woman who had stepped out from within the house, he continued to sit with his head bowed.

When he looked up and saw me still standing there, he jumped to his feet and whipped off his coat and tie in an outburst of anger. Preacher or not, my head told me to make a run for it. His body language had spoken some very serious intentions, and it did not include any message of "forgiveness is divine."

Up until now, I had yet to experience the hand of the Lord directly upon my person since baptism. I figured this was neither the time nor the place for that first experience. If this preacher wanted a foot race, I was more than ready for the challenge.

Native Americans claimed that the wind was fast because it was free. Well, my life had also evolved as a free spirit in the winds of nature, and it too had made me fast. No one had ever successfully run the rabbit down. And I was confident that any man of the cloth would be no match. They might lay claim to being fast in other respects, but a foot race would not be one.

Nevertheless, being exceptionally smaller than others of my age, every foot race became a serious matter when life and limb were at stake. And this contest had every appearance of being no exception. Wasting no time, I returned to the tracks to take the race to the country. That decision was by no accident. I was heading for the land that was like home to me.

Passing the first mile marker, I glanced over my shoulder to see if the man dressed in black was either gaining or losing ground. Running the gauntlet of jagged rocks entrenched between irregular wooden ties required intensive footwork more suitable for a surefooted mountain goat. However, being a preacher did not seem to hamper his ability to navigate the loose terrain.

These tracks marked the beginning of the marathon between boy and preacher.

Two miles beyond the marker, we reached the trestle extending over the Snake River. As the mid-afternoon sun continued to beat down hot rays of wrath, I slowly increased the pace. In response, the Preacher made no attempt to close the distance. After crossing over the trestle, I realized it would take more than just a long run on a pile of rocks to win this race.

As the sweat began oozing from every pore, I abruptly turned into a newly plowed field. I could see that the narrow groves cut by the plow shear were too small to accommodate a man's footstep. For the preacher to keep his stride on top of loose furrows would be like tracking through sand dunes in lead boots.

Half way through the field, I expected the preacher to gracefully bow out of the race. I was mistaken. Somehow he had successfully passed the test of endurance like a gold medal marathon runner. Whatever stubborn determination or divine faith he brought with him, it had yet to fail. But what he could not foresee was that the real race was only beginning.

At the far end of the plowed field, this preacher would soon discover a whole new set of challenges. A long, thin bog area of treacherous proportions lay ahead. I had every intention to carve a zigzagging path directly through the middle of the quagmire. If the preacher elected to avoid the treacherous crossing by attempting to circumvent the bog, he would not be fast enough to remain in the race. If he entered, the outcome would be uncertain.

With legs churning, I vanished into a series of low bramble branches determined to slap my face. Hidden from view and breathless, I stopped momentarily to inhale several deep breathes of fresh air. When the sound of branches snapping not too far in the distance announced the arrival of the determined preacher, I knew nothing had changed.

Lying before me was the most dangerous course through the bog. It was treacherous because it had an unforgiving attitude that did not take kindly to trespassers. Being familiar with this formidable landscape, I lunged into an entanglement of wiry brush thick enough to blot out the sun.

To survive, I had learned it was imperative to step carefully from one clump of roots to the next. Speed was not the key to success. However, failure to adhere to strict bog etiquette increased the risk of smashing through the top layer of soft vegetation. The result could be anything from a twisted ankle to deadly entrapment.

When I finally emerged, every part of my body was covered with the stench of decayed vegetation. My heart pounded so hard, it felt like it was ready to explode. With the river only a short distance away, I seized the moment for a quick plunge into the refreshing, cool waters. Crossing the river, I ascended the embankment to rest and secure a better view.

In those first few moments, I pondered on whether the elements would conspire to consume this man of God. During the race, I recalled thinking that the bog idea seemed like a good one. Now I began to have doubts on whether I had done the right thing. To survive the mucky bog required a degree of toughness and a little bit of skill. What would happen if the preacher failed to emerge?

For whatever it was worth, I was worried the preacher might seriously falter. If I had made a fatal mistake, would God ever forgive me? I was sure my parents would have a lot of reasons not to. The only prayer I knew was the one Mom had me say every night. It was very short and to the point:

> "Now I lay me down to sleep.
> If I die before I wake,
> I pray the Lord my soul to take."

When I heard the unmistakable slushy sound of footsteps crushing vegetation somewhere within the swamp I was relieved, for there was no way my evening prayer would have provided much help.

Perplexed on how this preacher managed to survive all the obstacles, I began thinking that maybe God had not abandoned him after all. The last remaining challenge would provide the answer. It was an expansive pasture with barbed-wire fences to hurdle, gopher mounds to circumvent, woodchuck holes to stumble into, slippery manure to slide on, and scattered debris to trip over. Mother Nature, with the assistance of man, had created an incredible obstacle course prone to causing accidents.

To be a survivor, one would require ingenuity and persistence. I could only hope that the final leg would prove to be even more treacherous to a tired and weary preacher. And although I had no desire that the preacher man become road kill, I was confident he would succumb to the elements and withdraw from any further pursuit.

Taking advantage of my lead, I rested for a few moments to watch this man of incredible endurance emerge from the bog. As he stumbled forward on all fours he no longer carried that shiny and neatly dressed appearance of a typical preacher. Covered from head to toe with patches of black muck ingrained in his white shirt and with hair rearranged like a jungle man from a Tarzan movie, he was a holy sight, but not in a religious context.

When he paused at the edge of the river, he took notice that he was being observed from afar. At the same instant, I wondered if God might also be watching. If so, would he favor an outcome? After several deep breathes of fresh air, the man charged head first into the turbulent water.

Moving a short distance into the obstacle course, I paused once more. This time it was intentional. To make the obstacles effective, it was imperative that the preacher man was just the right distance away to properly introduce him into the obstacle course.

When the preacher reached the fence line, he paused again, probably for a short prayer of forgiveness for what he was about to do. When finished, he quickly brushed over the fence and surged forward in hot pursuit. Half way into the field, I abruptly turned in my tracks to draw him across a selective plot of ground treacherous with gopher mounds and bad-ger holes. Spotting an opportunity to close the distance, he took the bait. It was a big mistake. He stumbled from grace and crumbled to the ground.

Heartened by the sudden turn of events, I paused to catch another moment of oxygen. Never far from my mind was what had motivated the preacher to pursue so relentlessly. But most disturbing was that I could not understand how a man of the cloth managed to survive so long.

By now, the exhilaration of the chase had begun to take its toll. The onslaught of exhaustion had settled into every muscle of my body. When the preacher man stood up straight, brushed himself off and continued the race limping with one leg, it was a bad omen.

In the final quarter mile, I felt more like a hunted quarry with an unrelenting bloodhound in pursuit. With the last of my inner strength drained, the rabbit finally slowed to a crawl. If God were watching, what a sorrowful sight we must have been.

Sweating uncontrollably and totally exhausted, my rubbery legs finally collapsed near an old tree stump. When I struggled to stand, my body refused to move. Unknown to the limping clergyman, he was on the verge of his own miracle. However, the sacrifice for his notable victory was etched on his weary face, tattered clothing, and a limping leg with a missing shoe.

When the preacher reached the stump he dropped like a stone. Despite his complete exhaustion, he managed to sputter an incoherent sentiment that I deserved a licking. But in the same fatigued breath he confessed, "I no longer have the energy or the will to do so."

Beneath the bright sun in the middle of a sheep pasture, two totally consumed strangers patiently waited for a supply of oxygen to return their lives back to some semblance of normality. The silence was finally broken when the preacher shared his admiration on how creative I had been in alluding capture.

In response, I expressed my own admiration on how relentless his pursuit had been. But, deep down, what I really wanted to know was his secret in catching the rabbit, but I was afraid to ask.

After another period of extended silence, he peered down with a questionable look in his eyes and unexpectedly said, "Can I share a secret with you?"

As his captive, what else could I say except, "Sure go ahead."

He then revealed that he had not always been a preacher. In fact, he had only recently been called back into the ministry. Six months earlier and for several years prior thereto, he played as an outfielder for the Detroit Tigers in the American Baseball League.

He went on to explain how everything I had learned naturally about running, he had acquired through training as a professional athlete. However, he was quick to assure me that he figured very few in the community were like him. And if I was concerned about ever being caught again, the chances were probably slim to none.

From that very moment, I had a warm feeling that I had discovered a preacher I could understand. He sounded like an everyday kind of person. Maybe someone I could even befriend. I crossed my heart and agreed to never share his secret with anyone. In return for keeping my part of the agreement, he would never share the circumstances of our encounter. I gathered from our conversation he was only a visiting pastor staying at the parsonage. Our paths never crossed again, and I found out that the girl struck was not his daughter. However, the girl might have been the other preacher's daughter.

If there was a lesson to be learned in this divine but brief adventure with the Olympic-running preacher, it was that one should never be too quick to pass judgment on anyone. Having lost the race to the preacher also gave new meaning to the term "never." It would no longer be taken to mean "forever."

The greatest gift the community shared was the opportunity to be a child surrounded by people who subscribed to the American Dream. With very few having degrees beyond the twelfth grade, success was stepping outside the here and now. I believe there will always be a crucial difference in how we learn from a book and how we learn from experience. Residents of this community had learned from experience what words alone could never have accomplished.

With an unwavering belief that they could succeed, they were willing to reach out and achieve the unimaginable. Ingenuity had been instilled in their blood. In the end, their determination and steadfast courage captured the American Dream. We who were born to that generation were rewarded by their wonderful legacy that eventually took seed and sprouted beyond their imagination.

None of us are born with a distinctive character, nor can this be discovered from the pages of a book. Character is something we eventually build within ourselves. The community of my birth nurtured a peaceful, harmonious environment rich in people with character. From their example, I learned that the opportunity to be whatever I wanted to be was always there beyond the imaginary fence that we often built for ourselves.

But, by far the most memorable gift will be the legacy of a caring community, the kind of community that would rally together to save the life of a little boy carried away in the arms of a vicious and wanton predator. For, without that kind of community, his dreams would have been lost forever.

# Chapter Four

# LAND OF ADVENTURE

C APTURED BENEATH A BLISTERING summer sun, the boy from the past has returned to peer over the vast horizon of his birthplace. It seemed like only a moment ago that he was a boy surrounded by friends. Now he stood alone one hundred twenty miles south of the Canadian border and twenty miles east of the Dakotas on the flood plains of the Red River Valley of the North, a place where the mid-summer heat created simmering waves of air to dance in perpetual motion along a flat landscape of endless prairie.

The land that once journeyed into a world of timeless adventures has all but disappeared. The boy's buried footsteps have joined a much older history of a land rich in black silt that provides a road map to its ancient past. As a prehistoric body of water, the land is known geologically as Lake Agassiz. But on this day, the landscape has shifted to the rhythm of farming.

Fortunately, all had not been lost. For some things in life there can be no replacement. Memory is one. In the mental images of the boy's past, he can still clearly visualize a land that spanned from one inviting river to the next. He recalls the prairie flowers and green grass that once brightened the landscape, and the morning breeze carrying their sweet scent to every inhabitant. He remembers watching the hawks riding currents of warm air rising from the ground and blackbirds branded with bands of red gathering on nearby cattails. It was a period when the bounty of the land had come to symbolize the grandeur of the time.

The overabundance of natural prairie during my childhood was compliments of a federal program known as "soil bank." It had been a controversial concept at the local barbershops and cafés, where news was dispensed daily. Washington politicians had voted to pay a yearly income to every farmer who elected not to plant their land. In the minds of townsfolk, the program spelled trouble in the making. With an economy dependent on agricultural sales and employment, the heated debate was whether the concept would inhibit financial growth in the community. Truthfully, the real crux was that taxpayer dollars would be paid for no work. The stench of political pork barrel hovered in the air. It was un-American, at least in those days.

Above and beyond the verbal controversy, there was a silver lining few had ever considered. The ultimate good fortune of a vast and open prairie of grasslands gave birth to an overwhelming bonanza for Mother Earth. Quick and resilient, she responded to restore a haven of prosperity for a wide variety of prairie inhabitants, including one small boy. With the transformation from plow to a bountiful ecosystem, the heartbeat of the land was once again measured in terms of its natural beginning.

As the fond memory of that distant past transcended back to the present, the silence was broken by the screeching cry of a hawk circling high above. Patiently I listened for the warbling twitter of the yellow-breasted meadowlark to send out its alarm, or the rambling chatter of Hungarian partridge scurrying to safety among the thickets of grass. Even the numerous striped gophers that used to stand tall and straight as frozen statues were gone. They had all disappeared like snow in spring.

The land of adventure is a story of discovery between a boy and the land he loved. A discovery that eventually evolved to define the inward nature of the man the boy would come to be. Whether he was exploring the river, wandering in a field of flowers, capturing the "O-ka-lee" shrill of a red-winged blackbird, holding a baby frog in the palm of his hand or climbing a tree so high that the distant horizon seemed to lie at his fingertips, the boy would learn to be at home with every living thing.

Within the realm of his world, home was wherever life found meaning. He would venture through life not as a destination, but rather as a journey from one endless adventure to the next. His soul marched to its own beat, a beat that proclaimed that all forms of life had a stirring experience to share and to teach. But from the very beginning, he would discover that not everything about the land proved to be jubilant. It had an ominous side, a dark secret known to those who shared its existence.

During the twentieth century, more than once did the sky, land, and water embrace like old friends at a reunion. When they did, they released the rivers across the land. As the body of water marched across the prairie to subdue everything it confronted, the rich black soil solidified itself and returned to the resilience of its ancient lake bottom.

My grandfather William became a victim of the river's rage. In an instant, the swirling waters swallowed his existence as he repaired a phone line. His body disappeared to the bottom of the Red River. The memory of that fatal day would

East Main Street buried in water in 1943.

remain forever. When the news of William's demise was delivered to the door by a messenger, Mom became extremely distraught

Tears flooded her face as she suddenly dashed out of sight to seek refuge in the bedroom. I was abruptly abandoned in a cold kitchen sink half way through my evening bath. And in that brief moment, an unforgettable dark void had taken control. It was as though my entire existence had been set adrift within the same desolate waters as my grandfather.

Normally at such an early age, the death of most anyone, including a grandfather, might not be remembered. But I had never seen Mom cry before. The combination of her visible distress, and her sudden abandonment became a lasting memory of the grandfather I would never come to know.

Fifty years later, prior to the largest floods of the twentieth century in the Red River Valley, Grannie passed away. She had never remarried. The timing of this natural disaster made

# NORMAN COUNTY INDEX

### IN THE HEART OF ♥ THE RED RIVER VALLEY

ADA, NORMAN COUNTY, MINNESOTA     THURSDAY, MAY 1, 1947

## W. B. Johnston, Local Telephone Man Drowns While Repairing Line Over River

A tragic accident took place last Friday afternoon shortly before 3 o'clock, when William B. Johnston, manager of the Norman County Telephone Company at Ada, was drowned in the Red River just west of Hendrum, when a boat he was using to string wire across the river, capsized, throwing, him and his assistant, Jasper Wells, into the water. Wells managed to save himself by grabbing a wire that led to shore and pulling himself in, but Johnston, who was thrown out of the boat farther away was unable to do anything in the swift current to save himself.

Johnston, together with Wells and Alfred Stene, were attempting to restore telephone service to points in North Dakota, whre wires across the river had been broken. The bridge at that point had been removed due to the high water, and they had gone to Halstad to cross the river, coming back on the Dakota side. The telephone line crosses the river about ten feet south of the Hendrum bridge, and with the high water there last Friday the line was only two or three feet above the water. They secured a boat and had made one trip across and Johnston and Wells in the boat with Stene on the shore guiding the wire, were making the second trip with another wire.

They were pulling themselves across with the aid of the wire that had been previously strung, when the current started to pull the boat sideways, causing it to tip and throwing both into the water. Wells managed to grab the wire, but Johnston was swept away from it by the current, and although only a few feet from the bridge pilings was unable to reach either the

Stene and Wells made their way to a farm house and notified authorities of what had happened. Sheriff Bang with several assistants started work at once to recover the body, stringing a net some distance down stream and then using boats to patrol the river with grappling hooks. Assisting in the work were Ralph Visser, Bob Larson, Henry Helweg, Otto Habeck Jr., Lawrence Keppler and others. All day Saturday and all Sunday morning the crew patrolled up and down in an effort to locate the body. About 2:50 o'clock Sunday afternoon the body was found near one of the bridge pilings, about 25 feet from where the boat had tipped over. The water in the river had gone down several feet from the Friday afternoon mark, and was only fourteen feet deep at the point the body was found.

Mr. Johnston was born April 20, 1880 at Ocala, Florida, spending his youth and early manhood there and at other places in the South. He came to Ada in 1913 and has resided here continuously since that time.

Shortly after coming to Ada he engaged in the auto and garage business here for a few years, and then entered the employment of the Norman County Telephone Company, a position he has held for more than 25 years. The past several years he has been manager of the company.

Mr. Johnston has been constable of the City of Ada for many years, being re-elected several times. He also served as relief man on the local police for some time, and also as deputy sheriff. He was a member of the Modern Woodmen, and served as secretary of the local

On November 27, 1913, he was united in marriage here to Miss Lucia Mayer, who survives him, together with one son, Percy, and one daughter, Mrs. Lawrence (Dorothea) Hovland, both of Ada. Three grandchildren also survive.

Mr. Johnston was well known, not only in this immediate community, but throughout the county. He was faithful in the performance of his duties and when storms interrupted telephone service, was always out with his crew, many times before the storms had subsided, to restore service on the lines, and it was while engaged in such work that he met his death. He was an efficient and capable workman and it was due to his efforts that the local exchange maintained uniformly good service.

Funeral services were conducted from the Methodist church here Tuesday afternoon, April 29th, at 2 o'clock, with Rev. David Achterkirch officiating. With Mrs. Howard Menge as organist, Mrs. J. J. Teters and Mrs. David Johnson sang two solos, "In the Garden" and "Rock of Ages." Many attended the service to pay their last respects and there were many floral and memorial offerings. Interment was made in the Ada cemetery, with Oscar Bang, Ray Betcher, Adolph Restad, Henry Tufte, John Nash and Walter Sprung as pallbearers.

The sincere sympathy of everyone is extended the immdiate family in their bereavement.

me ponder whether my grandfather's spirit had decided to return within the same flood waters to reclaim his betrothed.

As their graves lay side by side, submerged beneath the flooded waters of 1997, it was a reminder that the land will always remain locked in the history of its water. It had been a history that began more than a million years prior to the coming of mankind. People who have chosen to live with the dangers and bounty of this ancient lake bottom do so by geological consent. And although residents claim ownership to their land, the enduring truth lies buried deep within its mystical soil, a soil that will always move to the beat of its prior life. History will always remember the Red River Valley of the North as the lake that time forgot.

Undaunted by its past, the boy willingly accepted the land with its perils of cliffs to cascade over, rivers to drown in, trees to crash out of, and the miseries of poison ivy and burning grass that blistered the skin red. He even tolerated the blood-sucking leeches and their vampire cousins, the mosquitoes.

To the boy, the land was a haven for a young adventurer. In the process of his discovery, he would uncover a treasure-trove of human experiences that illuminated life in ways that ultimately defined the man he would become. Tag along on a journey through the eyes and memory of a boy where the distance traveled was measured in the thrill of the adventure.

It's a journey of endless encounters where dreams can be captured while drifting on a raft in a gentle current across a land of endless space.

It's the discovery of trees that could be climbed so high that one captured the sweet scent of nature's perfumes passing through the airways.

It's a sensation created by the rhythmic musical joy of bluebirds, robins, canaries, meadow larks, wrens, killdeers, doves, and Baltimore orioles.

It's an experience in a land where life's most simple pleasures become an everyday discovery.

The birth of a warm and sunny day always signaled an urge to escape in search of an adventure. And the winding river separating the green meadows was always beckoning for more company. It was not far from home, less than a block, to a natural haven filled with friends from the wild. Near the shoreline, castle-like cottonwoods stretched up and outward in every direction. Limbs sprouted large enough that one could disappear among the leaves and never be discovered. Climbing to a secluded, lofty limb, I could select the best-reserved seat to witness nature's wildlife.

Waiting for my arrival were the noisy sentinels of the forest. With bushy tails flickering and backs pressed against the tree, belligerent squirrels sounded the alarm with loud, continuous chattering. This relentless chorus of jibber jabber could only be equaled by the never-ending noise of the monthly Ladies Aid meeting in the Methodist church basement.

How did I know? Well, whenever I was grounded for not coming home on time, I had to suffer the humiliation of attending one of those dreaded meetings. Mom had no other alternative but to drag me along. If left home alone, she knew that within a given moment after her departure, I too would disappear.

Sadly for me, Mom never came to grips with the principle that telling time by the sun was not an exact science. Quite simply, I tried to explain that without a watch, there was no other way to tell time in the wild. Truthfully, even if we could have afforded a watch, it would have made no difference. Whenever I was captured in the rhythm of a seemingly endless day, it was so easy to loose track of any schedule. The silent temperament of the land and its untouched natural beauty made one feel that time was no longer of consequence.

Regardless of any reasonable explanation, there was never an acceptable excuse for coming home late for dinner or supper. She would say, "Rodger, as long as you live in this house, you have to abide by our rules." It was one of those canons of law Dad would quote from some expert in rule making named Hoyle. In fact, the way Dad used his name, one would think he was of some importance like Webster was to the dictionary.

Solitary confinement within the concrete cell of the Methodist church basement, surrounded by an undetermined number of women chattering, was by any definition punitive. With no place to disappear, I could only close my eyes and envision myself in a favorite cottonwood near the river listening to my bushy-tailed friends chattering.

In elementary school, we would lift our voices to the music of "America the Beautiful." The words spoke to the natural wonders of our nation's land. Its "spacious skies, mountain majesties and fruited plain" were powerful images. In comparison, the ground surrounding the cottonwoods was to me every bit an expression of one of those images. Sometimes a keen and weary red-coated fox glided over the landscape. Using his protruding snout as his second sight, he probed into every nook and cranny searching for a meal.

Down the distant shore, I often saw a masked bandit prodding the sandy waterline. Unlike the fox, the raccoon's second sight was in his fingers as he constantly probed below the water, searching for a tasty crawfish. In deeper water, a muskrat loomed silently into view like a piece of driftwood, causing the waters to part in a V. Using his small tail as a rudder, he navigated in a straight line to the nearest clump of weeds. There he paused to smell the news of the day.

From my lofty perch on the tallest limb, the view across the water was one of green prairie grass and blooming flowers that stretched to the distant horizon. If I listened carefully, I could capture the sound of the water murmuring an echoing message below as it whispered by to some unknown destination.

Early morning provided the best opportunity to catch the morning breeze. It was also a perfect setting to play the "Blind Man" game. This was one of those children's games where one could be free to try a new skill, fail and try again. No one was keeping score. The rules required both eyes to remain

The view of a lofty cottonwood that still remains today.

closed. Then, one would listen intently to every expression that nature offered.

The objective was to visualize from those sounds at least five natural inhabitants before you could open your eyes, sounds like the:

Chirp of a robin
Caw of a crow
Coo of a morning dove
Tapping of a woodpecker
Shrill of a red-winged blackbird
Warbling twitter of a meadow lark
Whining cry of a blue jay
Hoot of an owl
Sharp bark of a fox
Minuet rhapsody of a robin, canary, bluebird, or a
Baltimore oriole

But beneath the murky waters of the river, an entirely different world waited to be uncovered. Clouded from sight, mystery lurked in these hidden depths. Fish were abundant. We commonly caught them with worms dug from the garden. Some fish, like the bullhead, had a slimy, smooth skin. Others, like the large-scaled carp, were ugly with big mouths that functioned like a toilet sucking water when flushed.

However, in early spring we were treated to the most delectable fish in Minnesota. It was the god of all fish, the walleye. Even the Norwegians, of which I was half, favored this choice over their beloved lutefisk. The exception of course was on Christmas. Then every Norsekie was expected to pay homage by devouring lutefisk one way or another as a symbolic bite to their Norwegian heritage.

We often caught enough walleyes for shore lunch and still had plenty to bring home for supper. As for the taste, the sensation that comes from a fresh walleye coated in cracker crumbs and seared in the flames of an open skillet has yet to be equaled. But the river was also blessed with giant frogs, the legs of which were as tasty as pan-fried chicken. Unlike today, there was never a shortage for a hungry adventurer.

In fact, frogs of the whopper size were so numerous they sometimes congested the river pathway like vehicles in a big city rush hour. The robust leg of a whopper-sized amphibian had more meat on the bone than a chicken wing in a present-day Kentucky Fried Chicken. Freshly skinned, the tender white meat of a frog leg coated in flour, sprinkled with salt and pepper and then sizzled in a pan of butter over an open fire remains number two on the list of tasty memories. The bad news, these frogs have become a vanishing species seldom seen and never as large.

It was safe to assume that not every inhabitant on the river was as friendly as a next-door neighbor. By any defini-tion, the most treacherous predator of the deep was the notori-ous snapping turtle. Unquestionably, as a successful predator long before our ancestors came down from the trees some six million years ago, snappers were the ugliest and most intru-sive resident on the river.

Masters of the watery underworld, snapping turtles always lurked just out of sight, waiting and watching for an opportunity to snap an easy meal. Most disturbing was that they were not always particular in their selection of flesh. Indiscriminate, they had been known to attack dangling toes. And if a stringer of fish was left too long in one place, the snap-pers moved in and robbed the catch of the day.

On calm days, when the water became a reflection of the land and sky, one could catch a glimpse of the pointed snout of this ancient predator protruding from the water. Barely visible, his head rose just high enough to breathe and survey the water's surface for a possible floating meal. Then it slowly slipped away below the surface without a trace or ripple.

A good-sized snapper could weigh anywhere from twenty to thirty pounds and reach the formidable size of four feet in circumference. Like a rattlesnake, the head of a snapper would coil itself within the shell and then suddenly strike faster than the eye could see. With jaws like a steel trap, they were strong enough to snap a dry tree branch. Fortunately for his potential prey, a snapper's attack was restricted in two respects. First, the distance of his strike was no further then his abbreviated neck permitted. Secondly, his attack was limited to a forward direction much like the strike of a crocodile.

As for the demeanor of a snapper, he appeared slow and clumsy, yet he could be both aggressive and ferocious. One's first confrontation face to face was an eye opener. It put a

Snapping turtle.

whole new perspective on how one might rank oneself on the food chain.

A word to the wise, never underestimate his capabilities and always remain on guard. Pound for pound his silent quickness, a body of cast iron, and his bone-crushing jaws, made the snapper a triple threat. But the most disturbing thought was that a person could find himself on the snapper's menu. With one good crunch of his powerful jaw, parts of any one or two extremities could be easily ripped away as his next meal.

My respect for them became so compelling, I decided to enter into a joint business venture with these predacious flesh-eaters. At the age of nine, I had visions of abandoning my career in scavenging pop bottles from roadside ditches and peddling curbside lemonade. My aspirations were to advance to the occupation of wholesaling turtles. I had hopes that my partners would become headliners featured on local restaurant menus as soup of the day or a tender evening steak dinner.

The business partnership's mission statement pretty well satisfied the first law of the jungle, "eat or be eaten." However, I did add one additional footnote that said, "Better it be them than me." The relationship proved to be precariously friendly. Well, as friendly as one could expect from a partner with a shearing mouth designed to rip chunks of flesh with one snap.

Mom, however, was not as quick to embrace the same enthusiasm. I do believe her anxiety had to do more with the fact that her backyard had become the central warehouse for my new enterprise. Her once pastoral green yard adjoining the garden was transformed into a primeval scene with live, vicious predators. Maybe "apprehensive" would be more characteristic of the vision she had of her son's new partners. Whenever she attended to the garden, she was very careful to give them a wide berth.

Aside from the inherent risks, it was to be my first major business opportunity. And whatever foreboding thoughts may have existed between these prehistoric survivors and me, it was now history.

Throughout the early part of the summer, I corralled a nice collection of whopper turtles, waiting for those restaurant sales to commence. Then late one night lightening struck. August was our season for tornadoes. However, this time it was a strong summer storm that blew out of Canada. It rolled across the prairie with the fury of a cyclone. By morning, the snapper enclosures were shattered and scattered across the landscape. Mother Nature's wrath had released the monsters like a script out of *Jurassic Park*. The resulting consequences became a tragedy in the making.

Under the cover of dark, every lethal predator managed to crawl away into the neighbor's vegetable garden. They instinctively took refuge beneath her leafy greenery. On that same morning after the storm, the neighbor lady tending the garden ventured into her overgrown squash to survey the storm's damage. She was completely unaware that she was venturing into a trap orchestrated by several large snappers.

When she brushed away a large clump of green vines with her rake, she came face to face with what appeared to be a pack of bloodthirsty snapping turtles. In self-defense, one of the large snappers struck the wooden portion of her garden rake. The great force of the attack swept the rake from the women's hand in an instant. In response, loud screams of sheer terror echoed throughout the neighborhood.

Alerted to the shrieking alarm, every neighbor within earshot responded like firemen rushing to the city fire siren. Once they had confronted the cause of the disturbance, there was no doubt as to its origin or the responsible party. Unfortunately, this one little mishap forced a quick bankrupt ending to a potentially prosperous turtle business.

But in spite of our short relationship, I fortunately walked away with every one of my extremities. In addition, what I took away from the snapper experience was a more favorable understanding of fear. From that time on, whenever I was confronted with fear, I immediately opted to embrace it.

Prior to our business venture, I had been somewhat apprehensive of snappers. Now that I had acquired a measure of familiarity, the apprehension disappeared. The lesson was simple. Once I conquered the knowledge and limitations of whatever I feared, the power of its influence dissipated. Ultimately, this single lesson acquired from my reptilian relationship proved to be more important than any financial ramification.

I have often wondered why some people manage to overcome circumstances in which others fail and even perish. I still ponder that very same question whenever I reflect on my early childhood. With a fixed mind-set cradled in the unconscious conviction that in every adventure life was assumed to be a given, the real tragedy for me was not in dying, but in never living.

Buried in this serene confidence common in the exuberance of youth, I could never visualize the expectation of ever dying. It was not a part of the mental equation. It remained only an option patronized in movies and reserved for older people whose time had ultimately come.

Within this mental framework, the balance between peril and excitement perpetuated itself as the driving force behind every adventure. Even in the simple game of "Follow the Leader," a spirit prevailed to go beyond the limits with a reckless disregard of what could happen.

The objective of this homespun game was to choose a leader who was challenged to do feats of courage that others would be unable to follow. He had three opportunities to eliminate all who followed in his exact footsteps. If he failed, his leadership was surrendered to another. The language directed to everyone before each challenge began were the words "I dare you."

It would be difficult to imagine a better or more hazardous playing field for this game than an excursion along the river. Challenging hazards loomed everywhere, from unpredictable watery depths and currents, treacherous sand cliffs, trees, and bogs begging to be part of a dare. It proved to be the perfect natural playground where lessons learned would become lessons earned. Unbeknown to me at the time, some lessons could also prove to be permanent.

Crazy Mick was a fellow adventurer. Lean and wiry, he had a lot of gusto. His face was an eager one. He was likable, and always held himself out to be absolutely fearless. On what appeared to be his final day of judgment, he became a testament to his own enlightenment as to why some survive while others die.

Selected as the first leader, he intended to achieve the ultimate challenge. It would be a daunting feat to which no one would have the courage to follow. There were four of us that day who tromped behind in his footsteps, eager to accept his challenges. Yet, we were not following blindly. We were prepared for most anything. The nickname "Crazy Mick" was not a title acquired by accident, but by a reputation well earned from his prior goofy adventures.

Rounding the bend where the water swirled in a backwash, our fearless leader suddenly made a running jump into a pool of dark, mucky water. It was a leap of faith into a juicy mixture which up until now had been commonly accepted as a forbidden area. Not even the animals were dumb enough to venture into this bottomless pit of black molasses.

We referred to it as the quicksand of the prairie. Comprised of a mixture of rich, black soil from the ancient lake bottom and decaying vegetation, it created a thick, sticky and extremely smelly substance. And it was lethal.

Prior to his jump, with a firm upper lip, Mick announced "I dare you to submerge under this muck for sixty seconds." As he disappeared beneath the darkened waters, I replied, "Who would ever be that stupid?"

Everyone began counting to sixty. When the count reached sixty, Mick was still nowhere to be seen. At the count of seventy, a trickle of air bubbles began accumulating near the surface. Then like a cherry bomb bursting, the muck exploded to reveal a portion of Mick's ghastly looking face choking for air. Then both of his arms thrust to the surface. Frantically they began clawing to reach out for something, anything. It was a desperate effort to cling to life.

The situation was serious. With one or both feet anchored to the bottom, Mick was soon destined to be a "goner." This was a sinister term we reserved for such special occasions. I think it was intended to defy the threat of death as some kind of joke. My suspicions were that Mick had unintentionally slipped too deep into the black muck with his dramatic jump.

Instinctively, I flung both arms out and made a flat belly dive into the murky water behind Mick. Remaining afloat, I embraced both sides of Mick's head and began to yank as hard as possible. As I labored furiously, the adrenaline pumping though my veins began to beat like a jack-hammer. But no matter how hard I pulled, the thick, mucky substance continued its grasp with a predestined determination. It was a grip that felt like a welcomed hold to eternity.

Faced with the prospect that I would lose this tug of war, my mind began to flash in and out with a swirl of ideas. Sometimes one event can trigger a memory from an entirely different event. So it was for me. From out nowhere, I remembered an incident where I had rescued a mouse from the mouth of a snake. The slithering predator had already succeeded in swallowing about a third of its catch. And no matter how hard I pulled, the death grip would not release. However, when I slipped a pair of fingers between the mouse and the snake's throat, the mouse sprung loose.

It was a bit weird to think that such an experience might prove to be a possible solution. However, there was no time to ponder alternatives. Mick was about ready to throw in the towel. Sensing that each breath of air could be his last, I screamed for the others to help tug on Mick's arms so as to keep his face above the line to permit an occasional breath. This would set me free to begin plunging my feet down along Mick's legs. Hopefully, in the process I could create a vacuum of air and water to release the bottom's deadly grip.

Each plunge into the dark abyss was a chilling journey into a black, living hell. If Mick's fate had long been determined, I wasn't convinced. Sometimes things just go wrong. And when they do, one doesn't quit without a fight. We were locked in that kind of deadly game. But the zest for life was strong. Eventually, persistence prevailed and the decayed matter surrounding Mick's legs began to give way. With several additional deep plunges and some desperate tugging, his entombed body eased to the surface.

Mick's destiny with fate had been averted. Was it luck or was it preordained? As quick as it had begun, the death-defying ordeal was over. Once on shore, everything returned to normal as though the outcome had been a part of the game from the very beginning. If Mick had been alone, he would have perished. But he was smart enough to calculate that the odds were in his favor in the company of experienced friends.

Follow the Leader was a game based on a simple principle. If another person could do it better, that person became the leader. It was child's play back then, but it was another lesson never forgotten. One day I would discover that the simple principle would not be much different in the corporate world.

As a young adventurer, I was living in a land of dreams that I thought would last forever. But I was wrong. It could and did change in ways never imagined. New neighbors had moved into the old, abandoned home up from the river. They were quick to brand my wild friends as noxious pests. At first, they began to destroy the habitat by removing all the trees except the cottonwoods. Eradicate was their battle cry.

In one brief period, what was once a haven for wildlife was now becoming an extermination ground. Then one day from my perch, I spotted a mother cottontail strangled in the jaws of one their steel traps. Her newborn were nuzzling up close to her soft, fury coat. It was like they were patiently waiting for her to awake. They could not know her sleep would be eternal.

As I continued my vigil from the limb of the cottonwood, I recalled the treasured memory of this friend. She had lived in a burrow under the old woodshed. It wasn't a perfect home, but with a lot of care and love, she managed to successfully produce several litters of soft, cuddly descendants.

What made her exceptional was that she never appeared fearful of my presence. It was like she had some kind of sixth sense that told her I meant her no harm. I was even permitted to hold her offspring. Her tolerance expressed a special feeling of kinship. Now her fate had sealed the fate of her young.

Anger began to grow from somewhere deep within me. Climbing down from the tree, I marched up from the river to the back entry leading into the house. I was angry enough to tell these killers exactly what I thought of them. Opening the back door, I discovered the headless skinned carcasses of several squirrels hanging by strings from the rafters. Now I was really angered. My immediate reaction was that they had to go.

Later that day, I was playing with my friend Kippy when he told me about his older brother's new birthday gift. Terry had acquired an advanced kind of pellet gun that could be pumped up to create extra power. He said it could penetrate anything. I asked, "Could it shoot through a screen and a window at the same time?"

He replied, "Not a problem."

His revelation was an answer to my prayers. The riddle on how to remove the older couple from the river had been simplified. I would shoot enough holes in the windows so that the house would become too cold to inhabit. With summer gone and fall almost over, the expectation of a cold and snowy winter was drawing near. Therefore, they would have no other alternative except to leave. There was a certain degree of simplicity in my plan, but not much brilliance.

Sadly for Kippy, I convinced him to join my noble cause. I will never forget the evening when the constable came to the house and began talking to Dad. I had overheard the conversation from within my bedroom situated next to the back entrance. The constable asked, "Do you think your son could give us any leads as to who might have shot holes through the windows of the house down by the river"?

Dad replied, "I wouldn't know, but we can certainly ask him."

Walking out, I proudly announced, "I know who did it. It was Kippy and I." The look on my father's face was one of shock and disbelief. Then I went on to explain how these intruders had killed the trees and were murdering every living thing on the land. I just wanted their house to become so cold that they would have to live somewhere else.

Following my brief explanation, there was a long silence. Both seemed to have a puzzled expression on their faces. I thought I had given a thorough explanation. Finally, the constable cleared his throat and spoke gently to Dad, "Get a hold of Kippy's uncle, and the two of you do what has to be done".

Well, the old couple had won. Dad and Sarge ended up replacing the windows, and they stayed. As for my punishment, I was forbidden to ever go near their property again.

I did not know it then, but Dad's restrictions became a pivotal point in my future adventures. My journeys would now take me to the larger rivers beyond the fringes of town. There I would discover a new expanded frontier for danger and peril that would challenge the meaning of survival.

In the span of our short lives, I hope each of us will indulge at one time or another in creating a personal dream of paradise. Whenever I indulged in some form of fantasy, I was able to create an expression of resolve that gave purpose to my life. In my childhood, the unremitting dream of paradise flourished in the vast spaces of the country where trees, water, and prairie thrived in harmony. Admittedly, I was personally biased to the sensational image that came from water, especially rivers. For me, they provided the landscape with an expressive earmark much like the mountains are to the West. They were the secret portals to travel to distant dreams of untold adventures. Like the blood flowing through our veins, moving water disbursed and nourished life to both land and inhabitants. And those who could embrace its beauty, power, and emotion were also fortunate enough to share her secrets.

We dubbed one of our adventurous rivers "The Snake." Twisting aimlessly back and forth like a snake slithering through the grass, the river shaped and carved itself into a deep furrow. Of course, the waters also offered up more than its share of snakes, a second reason for its name. In early summer, nests of newborn garter snakes numbered in the hundreds. They swarmed from holes beneath decaying tree stumps to slip away into the sanctuary of the grass. I recall thinking at that age how unfortunate it was that school had been recessed for the summer.

Imagine how many classmates would have gotten a real scream from these little wiggling critters. Especially, if a hundred squirming reptiles just happened to find their way into the girl's bathroom. The scene would have been a title wave of bodies screaming and running for the exits. With total panic set loose in the hallways, the principal warden with punitive yardstick in hand would have been charging from room to room, searching for suspected culprits.

It was a vision whose time would never come. Mother Nature's reproductive clock was impossible to synchronize with the school calendar. All in all, that was probably a stroke of luck. I had a reputation of being a creative mischief-maker. With a principal bearing his own stern brand of corporal punishment and absolutely no sense of humor, a bruising clash would have been inevitable.

Beyond the reach of the rivers, much of the landscape was mundane. In contrast, near the flowing water stood the tallest trees deeply rooted in the riverbank. Other areas with bountiful, tall grass provided a natural habitat for prairie chickens, pheasants, and Hungarian partridges. Even the flooded backwaters that occupied the lowland were always filled with migrating waterfowl. The land had proven to be both diverse and serene for adventurers and wildlife inhabitants.

But the river's most enduring appeal was that it offered up a new challenge around every bend. Whether one elected to walk or float the river by raft or log, they were guaranteed the unexpected. On our long journeys, the convenience of a raft provided the pleasurable experience of lying on one's back as the rest of the world floated by as if on parade.

We fashioned our rafts from dry, weathered timber that had accumulated near the river or in adjoining wood lots.

Bound together by treated rope, a typical raft could accommodate as many as three lightweights. When the day came to a close, we simply retrieved our bindings and headed home across country.

How far we traveled in a day depended upon the adventures encountered. Of course, the typical hazards of floating debris, high water, and sandbars were always factors. Any traveler unfamiliar with the unpredictable river would soon discover that the waterway could be an unforgiving master. Strangely enough, the greatest exposure came from the most unlikely sources, such as a fallen tree.

We are not talking about some ordinary dead tree, but one that had fallen into the river with its roots remaining firmly attached to the embankment. If the leaves were still green, what peril awaited beneath the water was even more concerning. The danger of a live tree partially submerged in the river was that it retained a full compliment of strong and vibrant limbs above and below the surface. On the other hand, a fallen dead tree was likely to have all of its branches broken beneath the water.

Danger came from the unexpected reality of being forcibly grabbed and swept under the tree in a turbulent current. Like an undertow in the ocean, the suction created a downward thrust to the river's bottom. The real hazard for the inexperienced lay in the panic of unexpectedly being dragged beneath a live tree where a bit of clothing might be snagged. For those unfortunate souls, the river offered a watery grave.

Rightfully, these specific trees of peril earned the reputation of "death trees." Anyone required to enter the water to release a snared raft from the grip of a "death tree" did not hesitate to strip to the bare skin to avoid being snagged.

Fortunately for us, not all sunken trees, whether they were dead or alive, were dangerous. If they had been, I probably would have been a victim of the river long before now. Of course, dead trees were always less dangerous. However, both sometimes managed to fashion some sort of under passage for one to ride the river's gushing current. The sheer power of nature forcing volumes of water to submerge in gulping swirls only to be turbulently rolled back to the surface was awe inspiring.

One advantage of a "death tree" was that it could often create a deeper and more turbulent current. And when the right combination of depth and flow came together, the condition provided an endless exhilaration. In fact, it was not much different from a water slide fifty years later. The exception was that it had no fiber glass slide.

Sometimes life's mysteries have an unforeseen purpose waiting for the day to be revealed. In all the years I spent on the river, I never gave a thought to the possibility that my experiences with "death trees" would ever be more than just another childhood adventure.

Yet, twenty-five years later on a small, peaceful river in Central Minnesota, this childhood adventure would prove to be much more. As a proud father, I was eager to share the experience of communing with nature by rafting down a river similar to those in my childhood days. In place of a wooden raft, my wife Lynn, J. age eight, and Elizabeth age five, and I opted to ride inner tubes.

It was a warm Minnesota day with a beautiful blue sky, a good day to commune with nature as well as the past. The only things missing on the river would be the everyday sounds of motor vehicles, people talking, and phones ringing. I whispered to myself that this was going to be one of those exciting adventures into the world of the Boy My Children Never Knew. Never did I envision that it would be all too real.

As we began the float on our separate rubber islands, the signs of humanity disappeared. The towering woodland surrounding the edge of the river closed in around us like canyon walls. Patches of sunlight pierced through the branches, causing rays of light to flicker and dance on the moving but calm water. Even the birds cooperated as they harmonized in the warm breeze that carried a faint scent of greenery.

Elizabeth and Lynn were floating a reasonable distance behind J. and me. Midway into our float towards the entrance into the Mississippi River, the spiritual reunion with the past was abruptly interrupted. The current began to pick up speed. Immediately, I thought to myself that something didn't seem right. Rounding the next bend, the water began to churn. The rippling message instinctively sounded a silent alarm.

My eyes focused down stream on a fallen oak tree lying in the river with roots firmly attached to the embankment. The sight of a tree with green leaves above the water invoked an immediate response. I shouted, "J. get off the tube!"

He replied, "Why Dad?"

"Do as I say, and I'll tell you later."

I quickly ditched my tube and joined J. alongside his tube. Working in unison, we began kicking as hard as we could in the direction of the far shore. Brushing close to the outer edge of the tree to escape entanglement, my legs detected the strength of a turbulent undertow.

With J. safely ashore, my attention immediately turned to Elizabeth and her mother. Blissfully unaware of any near disaster, their joyful sounds of inattentiveness brought a sense of urgency I had not experienced since "Crazy Mick." I began shouting for them to get out of the river. But with the churning water and the distance separating us, my warning went unheeded. Rounding the bend, their tubes passed an invisible point of no return. They were on a direct collision course with the "death tree." I could not prevent it.

Instinctively, every part of my body and mind mobilized into high gear. Two of the most precious loves in my life were seconds away from the possibility of being consumed by a treacherous undercurrent. It was the same undercurrent that had pulsated to me a doom's day message. As I desperately raced along the shoreline, I could see Elizabeth was still wearing her brightly colored life jacket.

It provided little comfort. What had been intended to preserve life was now likely to become her nemesis. Experience was telegraphing an urgent warning to prevent Elizabeth from being towed under the tree. If her life jacket snagged on a branch below the surface, the force of gushing water would fill her lungs within seconds.

Once again, circumstances dictated that there was no time to contemplate alternatives. But time was not a factor. Deep inside, the answer had intuitively been retrieved and activated from a distant memory. At the very moment I reached the suspected "death tree," Elizabeth's tube crashed violently into the tree causing her to tumble head first into the water.

Lynn's tube had managed to bounce off Elizabeth's tube and circumvented the tree. As I sailed out over the surface of the river, Elizabeth had already begun her journey to the river's bottom. With one arm outstretched, my fingers barely caught the top strap of her life preserver. Attaching the other arm to a sturdy limb above the waterline, I anchored a foothold to another branch below the water.

Commandeering every muscle into service, I was ready to do battle. Could the boy and the man join as one to save Elizabeth before she succumbed to the power of the river? The answer was never in doubt. As I began to pull with the entire God-given strength I could muster, I discovered that the bulky jacket bucking up against the current gave an advantage to the river.

What I needed most was an added advantage that the river could not counter, something that was distinctively my own, like a surge of adrenaline. That kind of adrenaline the boy had used more than once to save his own life. Such a resource could only be accessible within the mind.

Closing my eyes, I focused on stiffening my resolve. It came as an angry, undaunted commitment that the river would never take my daughter as it had taken my grandfather. Looking directly into the fearful eyes of Elizabeth, I shouted with a fiery vigor, "Daddy's got you, and he's not going to let you go!"

The very thought of such a dreadful loss unleashed a divine surge of energy that forced the small life preserver slowly to edge its way to the surface.

In that brief moment, when tranquility had almost turned to tragedy, Elizabeth may never have known how close her wealth of time had come to being spent. I knew. I knew how powerful a river could be, how unrelenting and unforgiving. Later that evening, with all members of my family safe and comfortable at home, I reflected upon the day's events. I recall remembering how important the lessons learned from earlier experiences had been to avoid the loss of a most precious treasure. If I had not experienced death trees and what they meant, I might have lost a great deal that day, including, perhaps, my own life.

I also pondered once again the question that had remained unanswered when I rescued Mick. Does each of us at birth have a predetermined destiny with a physical address and a designated time? Or are we merely granted a specific number of free passes that we often refer to as luck when a desirable result is achieved? For me, the adventures and experiences from the land and river would ultimately reveal what I wanted to know.

There were at least three things to be discovered on any adventure to the river. One was about one's self, the second was the adventure, and last was the lesson to be learned. And while rafting down the river was an exercise that could be exciting and unpredictable, it was often a simple indulgence in peaceful solitude. In those quiet moments of tranquility, one could trace the path of a gliding hawk, interpret a cloud formation or even envision one's self in the footsteps of Lewis and Clark voyaging across the continent. As boy and nature melted together, time passed without notice in a world of hushed obscurity. And in those quiet periods of contentment, everything I ever wanted was within reach.

Some excursions to the river were well-defined expeditions in search of the ultimate, exhilarating adventure. One such adventure was called the "Bull-Run." Others might have referred to it as the "Suicide Dash." The game was orchestrated in Pasture Park, a grazing greenery designed by a local farmer. The barbed-wire fence outlined the side boundaries. The river defined the outfield boundary. The principal player other than us was the meanest looking bull roaming the premises. The simple rules of engagement were not found in any rule book. And I was pretty certain Mr. Hoyle didn't have access to them either. They had been shaped and perfected from experience. And although they were simple rules, strict adherence was imperative.

> Rule number one: First priority was to establish the fastest and safest escape. Preferably it was a high bluff in the bull's pasture where the river was deep enough to survive a running jump.
> Rule number two: Only one person at a time taunted a bull of choice. With the presence of other bulls, too much uncertainty came from the risk of multiple charges at the same time.
> Rule number three: When the bull charged, you ran like hell and jumped out over the bluff before you were gored.

A high embankment from which to leap far out into the river.

The consequence of having a specific set of rules in most games was that they were often ignored. This was especially true with an adolescent who believed rules were normally accepted as the exception. But when we considered the alternative of being gored or trampled by a charging one-ton giant, we had learned that rules could at times be helpful.

However, some bits of knowledge were not accessible for us to learn. Take for example: why would a bull be likely to be far more aggressive during the breeding season? Back in the dark ages of the 1950s, any understanding as to the concept of breeding or sex in any meaningful context was simply nonexistent. Neither parent nor teacher dared to embrace the subject of sexology. If one was to even utter the word "sex," it could result in a mouth full of soap.

To no one's surprise, very few under the age of twelve had any real comprehension of the subject until we were introduced to the colored pictorial depictions in seventh grade health class. Truthfully, they didn't exactly add much in connecting the dots either. It was like owning a car, but no one had the key.

Hollywood had successfully taught us how to become warriors to kill and conduct mayhem, but somehow movie censorship had been restrained on exploiting sexual content. The scripts were often loaded with suggestive episodes, but nothing educational.

I remember the Sunday when the Methodist preacher warned the congregation not to allow the flock's innocent to view the sinful movie entitled *Splendor in the Grass*. It was currently playing at the Orpheum Theater. A lot of good that sermon did. It only increased ticket sales by those bound and determined to uncover the secret revelations of sex. However, the only thing we uncovered was disappointment.

The objectionable portion of the movie did not live up to its billing. In fact, the controversial scene was more of a hoax to the unenlightened. Two fully clothed teenagers were standing and gazing intensely at each other within the confines of some very tall grass. When the music increased in volume, the grass began to wave violently as the pair disappeared to the ground. The rest was left to interpretation. I remember turning to my friend in the next seat and asking, "Did I miss something?" If this was sex in all its glory, something was amiss.

Parents were not much help on the subject either. They pretended to know very little, and what they did share was anything but helpful. The only wisdom Mom shared on the subject was the same advice given by her own mother. It was a simple warning that "You will have to sleep in the bed you make for yourself." That wasn't really a lot of help. It definitely did not provide any clue as to what we were about to experience from one mean, aggressive bull in rut.

When we beached the raft, spirits were high. The site could not have been better. The water below the high bluff in the pasture was sufficiently deep to survive the jump. With the bulls waiting in the pasture, rule number one was satisfied.

I had been chosen to challenge the first bull. The decision was accepted as a vote of confidence in as much as we were about to enter the domain of one of the most dangerous adventures on the river. With rule two decided, rule three was like playing in the ninth inning of a baseball game. You either win or lose.

The pastured landscape above the bluff resembled a picturesque park with large, umbrella-shaped oak trees. Beneath the canopy lay a rolling, green carpet dotted in a brown, blotchy pattern thanks to a lot of cow pies. Once everyone was strategically set in place, there was only one way out.

In Sunday school, the teacher impressed upon us the principle that, with faith, we could move mountains. I never took the teacher's claim literally. However, what I eventually discovered as an adventurer was that how I believed in myself was what really counted in getting where I wanted to be. Where I wanted to be now was ever so close to the largest bull in the pasture.

Two hundred yards into the field, I caught sight of an unbelievably large bull carrying a magnificent set of long horns. Standing like a giant in the shadow of a large oak, he was surrounded by several cows content to be chewing their cud. Each cow had an expression of confidence that suggested that they had nothing to fear under his protection.

Slowly everyone placed themselves directly behind me and the bull. In those final brief moments of tranquility, I seized the opportunity to slowly cross over to an open area baked hard by the sun. It was nature's way of creating a surface like concrete that would now provide a fast track to the safety of the river.

Halfway across, a reflection of sunlight flickered out of the corner of my eye. Slowly I turned and noticed that the bull had shifted from the shade. His large pearled horns were challenging the sun. I hesitated and stood motionless. The bull did not advance any further. Unflinching, the bull's small, round, piercing eyes were now focused directly on my position.

Unconsciously, my breath automatically shifted to a shallow rhythm as all senses sharpened to full alert. The aroma of fresh cow pies drying in the heat at my feet carried the precarious message that I was already in deep shit. For a brief moment, no one dared to move. The sun continued casting down rays of heat directly onto my body. With each passing moment, tension mounted as the sweat drained from every pore. By now, the others, secure in the knowledge that the bull remained attentive on the only one foolish enough to venture out into the open began a slow retreat towards the safety of the river.

Five minutes into the deadlock, my faith and I were alone. In a limited arsenal, I carried a pair of jack rabbit legs, the higher ground that provided a quick escape to the river, and the undaunted confidence that I could do it. With unwavering stealth, I advanced to the distance of a good stone's throw from a ton of hostile flesh dressed in a black, fur suit. They say strength of character can be measured in perseverance. If so, it would soon be put to the test. I slowly raised both hands above my head to imitate a set of challenging horns.

Meanwhile, the bull played the game like a good poker player. His demeanor did nothing to reveal his hand. When I lowered my head and begin scraping the ground with one foot at a time, the bull's tail responded with a quick flick like swatting an annoying fly. The rest of his body remained undisturbed. Captured in a dry and hostile air, I pawed the ground harder.

Bits of turf began to fly into the air. To add even more intimidation, I initiated a short threatening charge. It would prove to be the coup de grace. At first, the bull's massive body failed to flinch. Then he slowly and methodically lowered his head. His oversized front hoofs began to paw the ground with first one foot and then the other.

My every instinct was once again sending a telegram with an urgent message to run, to escape before the final charge. But I was determined to hold the higher ground for as long as he did. I remember thinking how courageous it was for a seventy-pound boy to face off against a two thousand-pound adversary. For a very brief moment, there was the illusion that the boy was in charge.

Actually, it was the bull that was in charge. All at once, the bull's head snapped up and with eyes ablaze, he let out a fearsome bellow and burst into a headlong charge. Racing forward like a powerful locomotive, he was laying down tracks directly towards my position.

Within the cavity of my chest, I could not help but feel a sudden coronary insufficiency. Fortunately, a flood of adrenaline gushed to the rescue. Energized, my legs churned in a hasty retreat towards the bluff. From the loud sound of hoofs striking the hardpan close behind, I sensed the bull was closing the distance. His unexpected rage and ferocious determination gave an extra sense of urgency. The notion that life can be played, but never won, was about to be put to the test. I had every intention of winning and living.

As we approached the bluff, nothing could have prepared me for what strange events were about to occur. With one gigantic leap, I flew out over the cliff as far as possible to the center of the river. Unbeknown to me, the bull had continued his pursuit in such earnest he was unable to stop his momentum. Consequently, he too became airborne as he catapulted out over the cliff.

Before taking to the air, however, his excessive weight had collapsed a major portion of the sand bluff, causing it to rip away from the land. Crashing down together, the pressure of two tons of earth and a ton of beast created the sound of a small bomb exploding beneath the surface. Above, the exploding elements sent a spout of water into the air like a volcanic eruption.

Fortunately, my dive had gone farther than the fall of the bull or the crumbling bluff. As our two bodies surfaced, the weight of the bull in the fast moving current continued to close the gap between him and me. Belligerent to the end, he was casting a few unkind comments with his wild bellowing.

With horns slashing from side to side, he was also signaling that he had not given up the challenge. But now he had crossed over into my domain. I was in control. In a current too swift for him to exercise any freedom to launch his attack, I quickly made a deep lunge towards the river bottom, swimming along the bottom to the opposite shore. The bull had no idea of my whereabouts. By the time I surfaced, the game had come to an end. The bull had floated down stream where he exited at the first bend in the river.

More often then not, the crises that challenged us in every adventure often became the mandate to override the inherent danger. Even when life was not more than a breath away from death, I may have measured the risk, but never retreated.

Sometimes I ponder whether the near-death experience on the bank of the river when kidnapped had ever played a pivotal role in my behavior. Maybe I figured that lightning would never strike twice in the same place. Then again, perhaps it was because danger and adventure have always been inseparable. What I do know is that the enduring appeal to embrace risk has shadowed my entire life. In fact, successful ventures beyond the boy's time would depend on it.

In the Red River Valley, railroads dated back to 1872. Trains were the lifeblood of the land. The whole economy of our prairie community owed its rapid settlement and growth to the railroad. Hitched to a coal-powered box, these monstrous iron horses were bigger than life. They captured the imagination of an entire population. Noisy and smelly, a train's immense power was embodied within a colossal maze of iron governed by a hard-ass engineer. He seemed to relish in the prospect of hurtling blasts of hot steam from either side of the engine's belly filled with boiling water.

The inducement and challenge to ride and play on these giants was irresistible to the fearless adventurers of the prairie. And as strong as the iron horse proved to be, it was nevertheless vulnerable. Jesse James on the big screen had proven that boarding without permission was there for the taking. Of course Jesse had the advantage of a horse, but we had the benefit of catapulting from the heights of a cattle-loading platform. In addition, we could easily breach security measures by a fast sprint from ambush along the grassy knolls.

In either approach, the key to success was to commandeer the train before it began to roll too fast. The second challenge was to avoid confrontation with the "railroad bouncer." He was also a conductor and easy to recognize. Standing tall and muscular, he sometimes carried a long wooden stick to beat bums off the railroad cars. Of course, his definition of bums also included little hell-raisers like me and my friends.

As it turned out, hopping a moving locomotive was actually child's play compared to playing tag on a moving freight train. This tricky adventure transcended all human limitations. It was comparable only to its sequel, the "Chicken Jump," a title reserved for our number one adventure along the river.

Conceived from the movie, *Rebel without a Cause* starring James Dean and Natalie Wood, it was the ultimate adventure. The game demanded the same unrelenting courage as exemplified in the movie. However, it was seasoned with a slightly different flavor for recklessness. Instead of using a steep cliff that cascaded into the ocean, our playing field focused on a steep drop from the railroad trestle into a treacherous portion of the river. The jagged rocks that surrounded the wooden supports provided no margin for error.

The focal point was directly beneath the center of the railroad trestle. It was the only place the river had carved a narrow, deep channel needed to survive the high dive. The alternative was to crash into the pilings of rock. As for the trestle, it was constructed of heavy, square, treated, wooden beams supported with long poles primed in the same dark oily substance. The entire framework appeared as a series of slanting uprights and crosspieces supported by several pairs of leg poles embedded deep into the riverbed. The rock pilings stacked around the legs prevented erosion from the current.

To be crowned a victorious champion in this game, one had to be the last to dive from the trestle as the iron horse came charging down the tracks. Positioned at the center of the trestle, the only way our feet could ever feel solid ground again was to exit safely down to the river.

What I recall most was that rush of excitement every time the train made its crashing approach. Etched in my memory was an understanding that the engineer could never stop in time. At best, he would only blast his whistle and blow a gush of hot steam. The engineer on the two o'clock train in the summer of the early 1950s blew his top more than once and probably in more ways than just his whistle. But, regardless of whatever efforts he pursued to intimidate those trespassing on his trestle, they were completely ignored.

The northbound freight invariably reached the river crossing at approximately the same time every afternoon. One hour before its arrival was reserved to practice our dives before testing our courage. The northbound normally carried a heavy load within the confines of a long string of rail cars clattering and banging iron against iron. As the hour of reckoning approached, a designated spotter was posted at a point beyond the trestle.

Placing one ear to the rail, the rhythmic clicking of iron passing from track to track would telegraph the message of the train's approach. Once the spotter gave the signal, each contestant carefully planted both feet at the edge of the trestle. With no way out but straight down, the last to dive would be crowned "top dog." The rest were deemed "chickens."

No one ever looked to know when the train was near. The low rumbling vibration, similar to a minor earthquake that vibrated the trestle was warning enough. When the rhythmic sound of tracks humming changed over to the loud pulsating beat of rail cars clanking together, the train had reached the edge of the trestle. At last, the blaring blast from the steam whistle signaled that the engineer was warning his annoying trespassers to get off.

In those final, desperate seconds, one's mind exploded with anxiety and uncertainty. The spirit within soared with a slight shiver of doom clouding the decision as to when to jump. Muscles tensed as they made ready. Then someone would scream the command, "jump." Like leaves falling from a tree in autumn, everyone drifted downward to the sanctuary of the river. The argument as to who hit the water last would come later.

As summer came to a close, the goal to be the undisputed "top dog" had been my elusive dream. When one factored in the physical limitations of the dive and the unyielding resolve of 10,000 tons of iron and steel, the answer as to how to snatch the title had always remained a challenge. But the glorious reward and the distinctive honor that would come to whoever succeeded spurred everyone's imagination.

By now, a pattern of behavior had begun to emerge in my life that was eager and confident to take exceptions to the norm. The inspiration was in part premised on the belief that with a little imagination, no dream was impossible. With that enduring thought, I was assured the title if I could only circumvent the danger inherent in the game.

When the day arrived for the last dive, I was prepared to do the unthinkable. Instead of making the usual dive to the river, I would dive to one of the square, wooden supports extending beneath the tracks. These wooden extensions were out about four feet beyond the trestle. In size, they were just big enough to accommodate one small-framed body. As primary supports, the evenly spaced timbers were much larger than some of the rest of the framework. Up to this point, no one had ever contemplated the possibility of seeking sanctuary on one of these supports as the train roared across in full throttle.

As seasoned veterans assembled for the final jump, the atmosphere was one of playful humor. No one was looking forward to the rigid regiment of school life. Utmost in every mind was who would grab the final glory of the summer. As the familiar roar of the two o'clock flooded our senses with exhilaration, we stepped to the edge of the trestle. I made that final glimpse down to the river. My focus was on the pile of gray rocks that looked like a stack of miniature tombstones. I knew what dead looked like.

The once testy engineer had by now become accustomed to our shenanigans. He eagerly signaled his own challenge with four rather than two friendly blasts of the whistle. Encouraged by his goodwill gesture, everyone seemed prepared to wait far beyond the normal time before making the final plunge over the edge. When the crucial time arrived, everyone but one sailed to the bottom. My small frame jumped in the direction of the nearest wooden extension. Landing squarely on target, my arms quickly embraced the dark, oil-smelling wood beam in a fierce grip of self-confidence.

When the entire wooden structure began to shake and rumble violently, my fingernails began to dig deep into the wood. Unexpectedly, the sensation I experienced was one of being violently tossed up and down. Nothing could prevent my body from becoming a fifty-pound bouncing ball of flesh springing up and down like a yo-yo.

As the massive iron monster creaked and groaned only a few feet away, the engineer blasted a stream of suffocating vapor with enough pressure to blow a full-sized cow complete-ly off the track. I could feel the hot air as it gushed through my hair. Fortunately, the wooden extension had been just low enough to allow the explosive steam to shoot mostly over my head.

My original intention of escaping to the river once the others had reached the channel was now clouded by more than just steam. There was a continuing deafening clatter of iron upon iron. The harsh sound was making it impossible to con-centrate. But I already knew the choices were not good.

I could either stay on my small island and outlast a thou-sand-ton train charging along at fifty miles per hour a few feet away or choose to fall blindly backward into a swift river encir-cled with jagged rocks. With a sort of strange detachment, it would have been easy to drift away and take my chances with a free fall to the river. But down deep, my earlier vision of tomb-stones signaled a message that this was not a surviving alterna-tive.

Dwarfed by the harsh clanging iron and steel as car after car violently jerked and collided together, I held on. Even when the sensation of strength began to wane from the pound-ing of iron deep to the bone, I refused to surrender. The number one commandment in every survival experience had been to "never give up."

Mesmerized by the passing rail cars as they sped by like celluloid frames through a movie projector, I failed to notice bruises were turning a summer tan to black and blue. But who cared? At that moment, the only luxury came from a deep breath of air.

Inspired by a spirit that refused to give up, I stiffened my resolve to persevere. With a renewed surge of determination, my fingernails dug even deeper into the wooden beam as my legs tightly grasped on for dear life with what strength remained. When the caboose finally passed from the trestle, the deafening noise was quickly replaced with a dead silence that gripped all my senses in a strangle hold. I could neither hear nor feel, much less dive for the title.

To claim the title, I rightfully should have already dived into the river. But the train was gone, and to do so would have been like crossing the finish line after the race was over. What would be the point? Those who had dived earlier would later comment that they had written me off as a goner. I would have never admitted as much. But quite honestly, the boy on the trestle did fight hard to ward off those same sentiments. If it had not been for the lessons already learned from previous experiences, I might have been a goner.

When the years of my boyhood ended, the land I had come to love had proven to be a very valuable learning experience. The land's challenges gave birth to opportunities for me to grow from within, to be brave enough to face myself when afraid, to be tenacious under stress and to be resourceful when life demanded it to be so. And that innate willingness to adventure beyond the norm would remain forever. It had been forged from a thrill-seeking spirit that propelled the boy to venture beyond his imagination.

Some might argue that the boy survived by sheer luck. I like to believe his adventures had nurtured a self-determined fate that could overcome challenges others were not willing to accept without recourse. His unrestrained spirit was forged in a belief that life's outcome can be determined by the attitudes that characterize it. He evolved with his own distinctive mark that would never accept defeat nor make compromise an option.

Engulfed in this sense of exuberance and confidence, life for him was not as complicated as sometimes it is made out to be. Consequently, he never felt helpless to change his own destiny. His fate was his alone to determine. As for luck, it was never an answer. It could offer nothing more than an excuse as to why some succeed and others do not.

But equally important, he discovered the value in understanding and learning the simplicity of everyday life. He rejoiced in the relationship that all living things had in common with the land. His spontaneous zest for life was forever captured within the song of a bird, the scent of a flower, the sound of a burbling river and from all the wondrous secrets he uncovered from his adventures within the natural world.

To Native Americans, the land was "Mother Earth," an idea far removed from white European notions of reaping benefits at whatever the cost to the land. The earth and its natural inhabitants have always thrived best when left entirely on their own. As man succeeds, the ecological environment tends to lose.

When we fail to recognize the intrinsic value of becoming stewards of the land, rather than takers, we destroy the dreams and opportunities of future generations. Ultimately what we learn from the experiences with the land, we learn of ourselves.

There will always be an important distinction between book learning and learning from experience. Both are important.

But one without the other is a deprivation of one's full potential. If we preserve our opportunity to engage in the unfettered adventures and experiences of the forests, waters, prairies, and mountains of America, we preserve an integral part of who we can be. It is a part that will reach out to learn. And in the end, how we learn to learn will make us more creative and adaptable to the changing challenges of every day life.

# CHAPTER FIVE

# LITTLE BOY WARRIOR

G ENERAL DOUGLAS MACARTHUR relished the belief that a warrior's creed was his sword, and his noble trade was the business of fighting. In war, MacArthur concluded that the warrior emerged as "one of the world's noblest figures." My early mental image of a warrior in war was a naive notion of someone searching for glory. But for those who were real warriors, war was more about self-preservation than seeking glory.

Yet, both the real and pretend warrior shared at least one common virtue: the need to be motivated with the knowledge they were fighting for something worthwhile. And once that priceless value had been identified, either style of warrior could rise from obscurity to the status of a gallant hero. In the forties and early fifties, Hollywood and the ten-cent comic book had unconditionally defined that priceless value as freedom.

World War II was all about freedom. We were the living war babies born when thousands of young boys were dying to ensure freedom for our future. How we would come to define

171

our own freedom would set into motion a course of events that would unleash a neighborhood war of unpredictable consequences.

At the time, I was motivated by a righteous belief that we were fighting for an honorable and noble cause. It was to be a crusade for the freedom to walk through the neighborhood without being threatened, the liberty to leave toys in a yard without fear of having them stolen or used without permission. And regardless of how pretentious these simple freedoms sounded in comparison to real war, they were nevertheless important enough to fight for.

My dad was extremely partial to Western movies and books. Religiously, he attended every Western movie, but he was not alone. More often then not I was in the seat right next to him. Mom had no particular interest in the violence of fighting and killing.

Beyond the theater, our entire neighborhood shared a similar interest in playing cowboys and Indians in the backwoods along the riverbanks. With improvised guns, bows, and arrows we assumed the identities of the likes of Roy Rogers, Gene Autry, Randolph Scott, the Lone Ranger, and Hopalong Cassidy.

One weekend, the academy award-winning movie *High Noon* transposed the real life image of a hero from the big screen into the mind and soul of a boy. But more important, the movie summoned a challenge for that boy to rise above the norm to achieve goals that, in the beginning, seemed unobtainable.

The Western focused on a small town and its marshall, Gary Cooper. On the same day Cooper traded in his tin star for the beautiful bride, Grace Kelly, the ominous leader of the Miller gang had been released from prison. Frank Miller's train was scheduled to arrive at the railroad station at high noon. Together with other members of his gang, they were prepared to vent their anger and revenge on Cooper. It had been Marshall Cooper who was responsible for sending Miller to prison.

The showdown between good and evil was inevitable. Having been married on that same morning, Cooper had a difficult decision to make. He could opt to escape from his past before the noon train arrived by running away with his new bride. Out numbered, and with none of the townspeople willing to help, it was the most prudent option. The other alternative was to remain and fight, which meant almost certain death.

I can still picture in my mind the scene as Cooper was dashing down the dirt road in a horse-drawn buckboard. His bride was still wearing her wedding dress. Suddenly, he pulled the racing buckboard to an abrupt stop. Turning to a confused bride, he said in an unrelenting tone, "It's no good. I have to go back. They will just come after us. We would have to run as long as we live."

Those courageous, defining words immediately imprinted a clear mental image that captured exactly the same dilemma I faced. Our neighborhood was under siege by the threats and intimidation of a gang of bullies. As I trudged up the crowded aisle after the movie, my mind began pondering that I too had to make a similar choice. I could either continue to run away from the present state of anarchy, or make a stand and fight for what was inherently right.

Suddenly, it became clear that whatever course of action I decided upon, it would define who I would be forever. By the time I reached the exit, the decision was unequivocal. The neighborhood had to be returned to unconditional freedom. Whatever the cost, I had to be willing to make the necessary sacrifice.

Americans who survived war understood the meaning of sacrifice. No war was ever a good war, but some wars had to be fought and won. World War II was such a war. It brought forth the best in us to challenge and defeat the evil inherent in some.

In that same noble vision, I was convinced that our war was to be a good war. It was not ambiguous about who was righteous and who was evil. It was simply a war to free us from those who had imposed unacceptable restrictions on our freedom. We had been born in the "land of the free and the home of the brave." Now the time had come to take back our inheritance.

There can be little doubt that what we read in the war comics, and what we saw in the movies played a profound influence on the war we were about to unleash. Hitler's war had come to an end. But it was only the beginning for the war in Hollywood and in the paper-bound journals.

I still relish the memory of action war movies like *To Hell and Back* with Audrey Murphy. As the most decorated U.S. soldier in World War II, his self-portrayal on the big screen as an individual with unrelenting courage helped define the meaning of hero forever. The euphoria of the American soldiers not only served as a catalyst that boasted courage, it also provided role models to personify. I would come to be more knowledgeable on handling a machine gun than how to handle a baseball bat.

One message became very clear in every war movie, one side had to be the villain. However, victory only belonged to the side of the righteous. World War II was all about the inherent moral right to be free from oppression. It was a concept that had always been the spiritual glue bonding Americans together from the days of the Revolutionary War.

Therefore, to be the righteous heroes who would eventually win the war, we would have to visualize the opposite side as the villains. It was a simple process of mental deduction, probably not much different from that of politicians who have urged their nations into war for millenniums. By some magical movie metamorphosis set loose within our minds, we easily transmuted ourselves from being ordinary to that of noble descent endowed with moral justification to make war.

One illusion of war we managed to acquire was the idea that the providence of God had to be on the winning side. As a child, I normally left complex issues concerning God to the expertise of our Methodist preacher. However, there were other influences beyond religion that had led me to believe that country and God Almighty were inseparable.

In 1861, the union army marched off to free the slaves to the battle song of "Mine eyes have seen the glory of the coming of the Lord . . . His truth is marching on."

The country's relationship with God was even confirmed by its own currency that explicitly recited, "In God We Trust."

If that were not enough, every morning before school we would stand at attention with our right hand over our heart and recite the Pledge of Allegiance. The Pledge singled out that deity relationship in the words; "I pledge allegiance to the Republic, one nation under God, indivisible, with liberty and justice for all." These words symbolized the belief that a liberty-loving nation existed under God.

As young, inexperienced combatants, we were not certain what part God might play in our war. What we did know was that the cultural environment had already reinforced the romantic notion that one should fight for both God and country.

Once we had embraced the symbolism in the deity of liberty and justice, an illimitable avenue opened our minds. It transformed the reality of war into a fabricated, illusionary fantasy. We reveled in the thought that we were the youth from the heartland of America marching off to war in pursuit of every patriotic value for which Americans had always fought and died. Unfortunately, such a departure from reality permitted our young, immature minds to become recklessly imaginative. Eventually, we would have to come face to face with the real consequences of such pretentious idealism.

As for the actual fighting, we accepted the movie conception of honor and bravery to confront an adversary eye to eye by indulging in individualized hand-to-hand combat. On both the big screen and in the comics, the war hero always engaged in at least one if not several individual feats of courageous personal combat. With that impression firmly stamped in our minds, hand-to-hand combat elevated itself as the preferred encounter with the enemy. In that setting, we expected to test our own personal skills against those of an adversary. The ultimate reward would be either personal triumph or painful defeat, but never anything beyond.

A further revelation of our own mythical image of warfare was in our weaponry. The arsenal we gathered was more symbolic than designed to do serious harm. Obviously any armament could cause pain, but none were designed to maim or kill. As for the use of these weapons, every warrior expected a good pounding from time to time and perhaps a few black-and-blue marks. However, no one had any expectation of being seriously injured or causing serious injury. There was no strategy to annihilate the enemy.

Perhaps the supreme fallacy of our notion about war was that every combatant would abide by the same unwritten set of rules of fair play in any engagement. Unbeknown to any of us, the day would come when the reality hidden within these fallacies of war would unexpectedly surge to the surface. When they did, it would change our young perception of war forever.

Who were these so-called "tyrants" of the neighborhood? From where did they originate? Were they really that bad? To be honest, the band of brothers we were about to declare war upon were not all bad, nor were they much different from the generations before them.

At the time, I would have fiercely disagreed with that conclusion. But ironically, I had a change of mind years later when I was practicing law in the similarly sized community of Long Prairie. There, I became close friends with the local jeweler. To my surprise, Richard revealed that his father, John Wall, had been in the jewelry business in the A.J. Johnson Drug Store on Main Street in the community of my birth. He would later move his family to Long Prairie.

Even more interesting, he shared the experience of his own battle with another young clan of brothers when visiting his grandparents. Strangely enough, they too wanted to test their own manhood as a collective group of bullies on those same streets I roamed as a child. My imagination was captivated by the coincidence since Richard was a generation older than I.

Richard described the occasion. Clara, his grandmother, had sent him on an errand. The closest route to the store was the sidewalk along Main Street. As he passed the blacksmith shop next to the implement business, three brothers were blocking the width of the sidewalk. That area of concrete did not have any particular significance, especially for Richard.

The same was not true for those denying him the freedom to pass. Apparently they had marked out their own turf and were eager to have someone test their resolve. Outnumbered three to one, Richard expected to lose this battle. But he was not one to back down. At least, not before he could manage to take one of the brothers down with him. In the course of fists flying in every direction, two big burly blacksmiths stepped out of the shop to intervene.

Both men had enormous muscles shaped and fashioned from bending and pounding iron and steel. One of the gentlemen was Mr. Neilson, the owner. The other was Andrew T. Pinske, Richard's grandfather. A few years later, he would be fatally shot in World War II in the battle for Italy by a German sniper. His name remains inscribed on the honor role at the local VFW.

On this day, his grandfather had no problem separating the young fighters. Andrew smiled at Richard as he turned to other boys and said, "If any of you boys want to fight, we are here to make sure it is a fair fight with one on one."

I suspect the smile was because Grandfather knew his grandson was a hundred and ninety pound center and linebacker for the local high school football team back home, and a potential all-state candidate.

When the ordeal was done and over, Richard said the incident remained a fond memory of the community and his grandfather, who, like my grandfather, had died before his time. When I grew up, I only knew these brothers as successful grown adults. Some worked in the implement business, and one was my dentist who also served on the city council for years. To me, Doc was one of the most kind-hearted and caring doctors I had ever known.

As for our adversaries, one family had five brothers and the other had two. They were not exactly the "Magnificent Seven," but the older brothers possessed more superior muscle power then the rest of the neighborhood combined. And when both families merged into a united force, they represented a formidable enemy. Fortunately, the two clans were not always together.

By comparison, our rag-tag force represented an undisciplined group of neighborhood children from various families. Our advantage was that we were more apt to use tactics that the enemy never considered necessary. In many respects, it was to be a contest between the courageously strong muscles of a confident adversary against a determined band of collaborators who hoped to deliver a creative and unexpected blow.

In respect to age, each family had a brother who was a little bit older and one about the same age as myself. These four presented an awesome challenge. They were strong, imposing and fearless. However, the remaining three were younger and more of a nuisance than a threat. We all lived in close proximity. The clan's domicile just happened to be situated in the adjoining block which some referred to as "shanty town." And although neighbors wanted to believe we were a step up from that block, I never made that distinction and, apparently, neither did the rest of the community.

In fact, that sentiment was later confirmed at my fortieth-year class reunion. I asked Jan, who was my first date ever, "Would you have accepted my invitation to the sock hop if I had lived in the little house on the south side of town?"

Her response was quick and forthright, "Absolutely not."

Until then, I had never given it a thought when the family moved to Jamison Drive. It apparently proved to be more than just symbolic.

The home Grandfather and Dad constructed after my parents were married.

Like most wars, the issue was all about territory, basically, simple geography. Whenever anyone from that adjoining block wanted access to the rest of the community, the only passage was through our neighborhood. With a river to the east, the fairgrounds bordering on the west and open country to the south, there was no other option to access the town except through our neighborhood.

As a general rule, our adversaries inevitably traveled through the territory on foot in groups of three to five. With the aura of authoritarian aristocrats, they intimidated whoever they encountered. By their unrestricted use of our toys or joy riding on our bikes at their pleasure, they had seized both an emotional and physical dominion over the neighborhood.

Eventually, the very presence of the clan caused neighborhood children to cease playing and scatter for cover. Even a self-proclaimed warrior like myself traveled off the beaten path to avoid confrontation with the clan. Someone once defined war as an "act of violence whose object was to constrain the enemy." Well, if war was required to constrain the clan, then war would be our price for freedom.

But before any war could be launched, provisions had to be made or acquired. In most wars, the ratio of non-combatants outnumber the fighting combatants by ten to one. We were not afforded the luxury of outside assistance or the benefit of financial funds. Therefore, we had to rely on our own creative ingenuity to improvise weapons and build our own defenses.

Our first task was to select and construct several strategic fortifications away from home. We had no illusions that if there was to be any fighting, it had to take place far from our own backyards. It was imperative that parents had no knowledge of our war. They had just experienced the brutality and tragedy of World War II. The very notion of children making war on each other would have been painful. By the same token, if they learned of our intentions, it could have proved painful in other ways.

After a little preliminary planning, the decision was made to fortify two primary locations. One location was a wooden shed next to an open field towards the fairgrounds. Abandoned for years, the solid wooden structure with a dirt floor had the advantage of no windows or doors. It was a hideout for older boys like my brother to secretly smoke cigarettes. The only entrance was a trap door in the corner of its flat roof. Defending a fortification from ten feet in the air provided a distinct advantage. In addition, if a battle spilled over to the open field, we could engage without interference from the neighborhood residents.

In a relatively short period, we had reinforced the walls with old boards scrounged from the neighborhood. When the fortification was finished, we celebrated by roasting hotdogs and marshmallows over an open fire on the dirt floor.

The other fort was near the river. It not only provided a sanctuary close to an area we spent most of the summer, but it was completely out of sight and sound of the neighborhood.

The location was a small island that extended out from the river near a large cottonwood grove. The island had the unique advantage of being long and narrow. And although water normally subsided to a low level on the far side by mid summer, enough water still remained to create a mucky bottom that would serve to slow any rear assault. The real strategic advantage came from the two large cottonwood trees. Their massive, protruding limbs provided a natural umbrella-like barrier against flying rocks

As soon as the mundane work of fort building was completed, we began assembling an arsenal of weapons, limited to whatever Mother Nature could offer. Like Native Americans, we were depended on Mother Earth to provide most of the needed materiel for war.

The slingshot was my personal choice. To be an accurate missile launcher, it had to be engineered to the right size and shape. I remember taking great pride in whittling the armament that would eventually help me level the battlefield when outnumbered or outmuscled. During the period of the little boy warrior, I never traveled without several precision stone cartridges in one pocket and my hand crafted oak slingshot in the other pocket. It would prove to be a most decisive weapon.

Another favorite weapon of choice was the hard oak staff. It could delivery a powerful blow with a mighty long reach. Forty years later, the habit of toting an oak staff still remains whenever I journey through the forest. Today, it serves as an effective support for walking. In those earlier years, such a weapon aroused a conviction that one was a dangerous adversary to be reckoned with.

From the river's edge, we converted strong willow saplings into whips, and, of course, we always had stones in our arsenal. Within two labor-intensive weeks, we had constructed enough weapons to adequately supply both fortresses. To be extra cautious we also hid caches of weapons in several secret locations. From there they could be retrieved in an emergency.

In retrospect, there was an interesting paradox in our construction of armaments. While we utilized knives and axes to shape and perfect our arsenal, we never gave a thought to using them as weapons. Of course, slingshots, willow whips, and oak staffs were not ordinary, safe toys. Nevertheless, to be stabbed with a knife or to receive a hard blow from a heavy metal ax would have been far more life threatening.

To this day, I have no clear explanation as to why such actual weapons were never considered instruments of our war. Maybe the reason had to do with our fantasy of a war where no one expected to die or be seriously injured. Then again, maybe this was where the intervention of God had come in. If so, parents would have been most appreciative to know that their persistent enforcement of regular attendance in Sunday school and church had not gone in vain.

In the final analysis, war preparations actually provided an unexpected measure of education that went far beyond the normal classroom. We were not learning the ups and downs of life from the pages of a book. We were experiencing them in a real-life setting. A place where everyday challenges became a catalyst that set in motion the energy to be creative and imaginative.

If we were to have any chance of succeeding, we had first to learn how to believe in ourselves. And how that belief eventually matured would ultimately get us to where we wanted to be. Fortunately, we eventually would receive some unexpected help from an individual renowned in his ways.

Some lessons in life are best learned beyond the textbook. Preparation for war nurtured a process of thinking that helped to change me forever. Tactical planning and conspiring became an everyday experience. Hopelessly outnumbered, our future was dependent on how resourceful we could become. It was to be a contest of mind over muscle. We simple had to outmaneuver the enemy strategically on our terms.

But the nagging question that kept begging for an answer was whether we could formulate a plan for victory. Were we just a bunch of dreamers, or could we actually pull this off? Planning and initiating our first engagement was to be a litmus test to answering that question. In hopes of a victory, we began an early campaign to recruit friends and relatives from all over the community. Fortunately for us, kids were always looking for a little action in the summer. They were not always particular on the specifics as long as one did not omit the element of excitement.

Back then, the community did not have a swimming pool, and organized activities were limited pretty much to sports. So when we sent out the call to join our freedom march, no one knew for sure what it meant, but it sounded good. Surprisingly, a multitude of curious volunteers responded. In fact, the gathering was beyond expectations. It had all the earmarks of an exciting celebration like Halloween night.

At first, when marchers began to mingle along the street, clan members mocked and attempted to intimidate the early recruits. One of them remarked, "Fat chance this is going anywhere." But as the numbers swelled, a change in attitude prevailed.

When I entered the street and shouted, "Are we going to take this?" the crowd replied with a loud "NO!"

Humbled by their response, the clan unexpectedly turned and began a slow retreat towards home. Faced with the prospect that the numbers were not in their favor, it was the right decision.

However, the mood of the crowd was eager for more excitement. The idea of simply walking away was not acceptable. Then someone shouted, "Let's get them."

Now that was an arousing challenge that went over in a big way. It had not been part of the script, but it was effective. Everyone responded by dashing off in hot pursuit like a pack of greyhounds chasing a brood of rabbits.

Sensing the electrified energy in pursuit, the enemy scrambled into the sanctuary of their two-story abode. The spontaneous, newly fledged warriors encircled the house. The general consensus of those gathered was that an enemy who capitulated without a fight was not good enough. Victory could not come without some kind of resolve.

When their mother appeared at the front door, jubilation arose from the marchers. Her presence was interpreted as some kind of sign that they would formally surrender. However, she did not come out carrying a white flag. She did carry a tongue that was more belligerent than humble. In no uncertain terms, she proceeded to scream out nasty words of wrath. The gathering responded by drowning her words in loud jeers.

A few minutes later, the mother appeared again and shouted, "If you don't get the hell out of here, I will call the constable."

We already knew that was not likely. Someone had already cut the phone cable. Brave in that knowledge, the response was a loud, clear chant. "No, no, no." I was not sure who had cut the wire. I suspected it had been the son of the constable. He no doubt anticipated that someone inside might eventually resort to calling his father.

By now, the mood of the marchers had reached electrifying heights. They had every intention to hold fast with no retreat until the enemy conceded to at least one of their demands. However, after an hour of loud demonstrations, it was clear that no concessions or any surrender was forthcoming.

The emotion I felt on that day superseded every expectation of a victory. It was much more than just humbling an adversary. The day had demonstrated that the reign of the bully could be broken. The proof was evident by the clan cowardly hiding in their home.

For the first time, I realized the enemy had entered into a battle they could not win. They were fighting more than a bunch of neighborhood kids; they were fighting American tenacity embroiled in the ideals that freedom could triumph over all the odds. As rookies, we had uncovered a newly found faith within our consciousness. It would never be tampered with again.

When the victorious warriors assembled to depart, the lookout posted at the end of the block signaled trouble was coming. That trouble was in the form of the constable. In an instant, everyone scattered for cover. No doubt the noisy commotion had caused a disgruntled neighbor to phone in a complaint to the law.

Securely hidden on the roof of a nearby garage, I anxiously waited for the constable to make his move. To my surprise, the man with the badge never attempted to enter the block. Instead, he motored ever so slowly past the intersection. I was certain he knew what mischief was afoot. Yet, it was somewhat puzzling why he did not attempt to intervene. Perhaps he was allowing neighborhood justice to run its own course, or maybe he knew his or the sheriff's son might be involved.

For whatever reason, victory could not be denied. As soon as the law had departed, we reassembled and gloriously marched back to where we had begun. We wanted everyone to take notice that a new day had dawned. We were publicly declaring our own Declaration of Independence.

That first encounter was more than a symbolic victory. In retrospect, it had inspired a new sense of confidence. And although we were under no illusion that one encounter could win a war, a period of peace did reign for two weeks without any incidents. Deep inside, I was hopeful that conditions in the neighborhood were about to change for the better. Confident in this new sense of security, I set off early one morning to inspect our fort by the river.

An early Minnesota morning after a gentle rain can be beautiful to behold. Cooler air lifted itself on a warm breeze, birds like the Baltimore oriole, red robin, blue bird, yellow canary, and wren harmonized from thickets, and the fragrance of wildflowers beg for attention. It was my favorite time of the day. I loved to climb a favorite cottonwood tree to watch the morning sun launch an assault upon the landscape beyond the river.

However, on this particular morning, I was on a specific mission to check the narrow footbridge leading to our island fortress. After a rain, the river would often rise and wash away our bridge supports along the shoreline. Standing my lever-action Red Ryder BB gun upright against the old cottonwood tree on the riverbank, I rescued two of the long wooden poles that had been set adrift.

Once the poles were reattached by tying pieces of rafting rope, I crossed over to check the fort on the island. Examination revealed no sign that the enemy had tampered with the structure. I was certain that the clan was bound to retaliate after their humiliating experience. I just didn't know where or how. Halfway back across the bridge, I saw trouble waiting on the far shore. Kelly, the second oldest member of the clan, was standing firm with my gun clutched in his hand. Of all my possessions, which were very few, I prized most my Red Ryder BB gun.

Kelly had silently slipped out of nowhere. Dressed only in shorts with no shirt and stranded in the middle of the river, I was in serious trouble. Showing no fear, I confidently demanded that he drop my rifle. His only response was to stare with a quiet, menacing air of indifference. He wanted me to know that he was the one in control.

Then he cocked the silver lever and fired two copper volleys in succession. Both pellets impacted the flesh of my left leg and buried themselves deep into the muscle. No experience quite equals the first time you are shot. In an instant, pain brought my entire sensory system to a complete halt. Blood began to ooze and trickle down the length of my leg. All I could do was to grind my teeth tightly together to prevent an outcry of pain.

With no place to hide or run, my mind was bouncing between pain and the formulation of a plan. It was safe to assume that the enemy would soon inflict additional injury if I hesitated too long. As the pain began to be replaced with sheer rage, I finally accepted the realization that the enemy had actually shot me. I would have never used a gun to shoot anyone. The indignation that someone could shoot an unarmed person in cold blood, beyond the movie screen, flooded my mind like water bursting from an open fire hydrant. Suddenly, an intensified level of anger I had never experienced before poured out from deep within.

Staring my adversary face to face only a few yards away, I stretched out the arm holding my hunting knife high into the air and let out a hair-raising scream, "Drop my gun or be prepared to die." Of course, I had no intention of inflicting harm, but I didn't want Kelly to know that.

Like a raging bull I charged towards the shore. Irrespective of the excruciating pain, every muscle in my body was committed to a banzai frontal assault. Poor Kelly was caught completely off guard by such a crazy, suicidal response. Uncertain of his own fate, he unexpectedly turned and darted off like a hunted rat at the local dump.

I followed in hot pursuit with the intention of retrieving my trusty BB gun and maybe a flickering thought of a little revenge. But within a block of the chase, he wisely ditched my most favorite treasure. With the gun's recovery, any further interest in pursuit quickly diminished.

As the excitement of the encounter subsided, so did the rush of adrenaline. However, the excruciating pain from two copper pellets lodged somewhere between the bone and outer skin had awaken. Retreating to the sanctuary of the river, I took no comfort in knowing that the copper had to be flushed from the wounds. Building a fire to sterilize my steel blade would be the easy part of the process.

Pinching down hard between the thumb and the forefinger on the bloody flesh above the open hole, I slipped the point of the blade behind each pellet. As soon as the copper was removed, I heated the blade even hotter to sterilize and bring a tearful closure to the bleeding wounds. The nauseating smell of singeing flesh was a lasting remembrance of my foolish blunder.

Sometimes in our adventures, drastic conditions required drastic solutions. In this instance, returning home with two bleeding gun wounds was not an option. Mom could never handle a son being shot, even with a pellet gun. Under these circumstances, she would always become a visionary who pictured different scenarios like eyes being shot out or something even worse.

Children have always understood that truth had to be shared with parents in a way that brought a solacing response. For example, Mom would be more understanding if she thought that my leg had been punctured while running.

She was well acquainted with my injuries related to running. A lecture by her on the wisdom of using care in running would bring a sense of finality to her responsibility as a parent.

Fifty years later, the lever action Red Ryder has not been lost or forgotten.

And after a few words of loving advice, she could walk away confident in the knowledge that her advice might prevent a similar incident in the future. Whereas, any notion of war or being shot would simply devastate the esteemed virtue of motherhood; the recovery from which might take weeks, or even worse, bring the war to an instant end.

In the days that followed, my friends and I found ourselves entangled in a variety of skirmishes. However, no engagement would be more physical and unpredictable than the "Battle of the Lion-Heart." In nature, few animals can withstand the ferocious fury of an adult male lion in his prime. In memory of this same ferocious spirit, I want to share a true story on how we adopted a community "social orphan" who would earn his metal of honor on the battlefield.

The incident began late one afternoon. We had received reliable reports that the clan was planning to attack the fort at the river. With such short notice, we found ourselves with a force of little consequence to engage the clan. Sam, our second commander and a few others were on a Boy Scout camping trip. What forces remained were young and too few to repel an enemy intent on launching a full-scale attack.

Every good leader not only needed to know when to fight, but also when it was prudent to retreat. The enemy had already exercised that wisdom. Faced with the prospect of a serious pounding, I decided if we could not find additional help we would have to abandon the fort. It was a gloomy moment. All our hard work would soon be trashed. As I departed, everything seemed hopeless. Then a miracle appeared on the horizon.

Like Moses coming out of the wilderness, a savior rounded the corner of the block on his bicycle. And although he was not exactly a divine deliverer in the biblical sense, he was a deliverer of the evening newspaper. If anyone could lead us out of our bondage with a victory over the enemy, it was this paperboy. However, it would take a second miracle to convince him to join our cause.

At this point, we were desperate. Faced with the prospect of a terrible pounding or retreating, there was absolutely nothing to lose in requesting or even begging assistance. Everyone on the playground at school was well acquainted with the reputation of this paperboy. As for any fighter, reputations had to be earned. Forged in blood more than once, he was regarded as one of the toughest fighting machines around. Among contemporaries, he stood alone as the fiercest. His name was Mike Running.

Mike, like the older brothers in the clan, had strong, athletic features that had matured early from a rough beginning. He was undisputedly the best of the best. Anyone dumb enough to challenge Mike was short on brainpower.

I can recall a specific incident during noon recess in grade school. The playground extended for a block on either side of the school. The new senior high had not been finished, so grades one through twelve were still together. Consequently, children of different ages played or hung around in specific areas that offered different activities. That is everyone but one.

Mike had pretty much marked his own turf. He didn't like to be annoyed. And most everyone knew better than to infringe on his private domain. Mike appeared to be at his best whenever he could drift into a state of peaceful non-existence. Yet, that proved to be difficult. He may have not looked for trouble, but it seemed to find him wherever he went. Especially in the context of untested males that were anxious to prove their own invincibility.

On this particular noon break, two older boys had joined together to challenge Mike. As they approached, Mike remained calm and gave the appearance of a lack of interest. When the two crossed that imaginary no-trespass boundary, they were greeted with an explosion of fists flailing and elbows flying. In seconds, one aggressor fell to the ground. The other slunk away with a bloody nose and a black eye.

If there was any chance to reach Mike, I had to be straightforward and sincere. His father had abandoned his family, and Mike had lived a difficult and troubled life coming from what people described as a broken home. Because of his reputation, he had managed to keep a respectable distance from everyone.

When he parked his bike to make a delivery, I started up a conversation. I quickly explained our desperate situation. We were simply outnumbered. And if we could not find help, bullies from the neighborhood would soon trash our fort by the river. Mike never had much talk in him, but he listened intently. When I finished, he looked me squarely in the eye and, with no hesitation, said, "Sure, why not?"

To this day, I am still uncertain why Mike decided to join our fight. He had nothing to gain. I knew that he understood the feeling of being an underdog better than anyone. He had always been a loner who had engaged in battles at home, school, and elsewhere. I am not sure if he ever had a friend. Trouble had been his constant companion.

But I believe we had at least one thing in common. He may never have won all of his fights, but he never cried. After the emotional episode of being kidnapped, I never cried in sorrow again. In contrast, I could still shed tears of joy. And maybe Mike could do the same if he ever had something to be joyful about.

The two of us rushed back to the fort just in time. As Mike removed his shirt, we were caught in a hailstorm of rocks dropping from the sky. The enemy was testing our strength. The strategy to locate the fort beneath two large cottonwood trees had paid off in big dividends. Much of the bombardment crashed into the upper limbs of the tree and fell harmlessly to the ground.

When the clan changed tactics to outflank our water defenses, I turned to Mike and pointed to the vulnerable spot where the full force of the enemy would likely launch their attack. True to my prediction, the hostiles screamed into battle formation along the river and charged towards what was assumed to be our weakest position.

In response, Mike seized the moment and pounced atop a nearby rock. Strutting high and defiant in plain view, his arms bulging with muscles like Popeye the Sailor, he presented a very commanding presence. From beneath his tangled hair, he was eyeball to eyeball with the enemy glaring fear into their eyes. At first, it took a few moments for the opposition to realize who was standing before them like a stature of iron. When that realization finally came, the once eager sounds of the battlefield fell deathly silent. I was a bit perplexed as to whether the attackers were really scared or just contemplating how to regroup for a different attack.

As tension reached a critical point, it became evident that the enemy was beginning a slow, but deliberate, retreat. Apparently, the tough fighting spirit of our adversaries had found its limitation. Unexpectedly, we found ourselves on the eve of another victory without any casualties. Only minutes earlier, we considered ourselves doomed to a bloody defeat. However, the battle was not over for Mike, for he had not yet begun to fight.

With a deep roar, Mike sprang down from the rock and charged directly into the line of the enemy. Like a furious male lion, he knocked heads with the eldest of the clan. Mike's entire demeanor had shifted to a raging feeding frenzy hungry to devour an enemy he never knew. The total surge in energy was awesome. Such exuberant bravery left us no alternative but to follow his exhilarating example. Shouting the command to charge, we all blitzed forward onto the battlefield kicking and swinging.

In the book entitled, *The Warriors*, by J. Glenn Greg, the author formulated three universal appeals that individuals experience in battle. One appeal was the delight in seeing; a second was the delight in comradeship; and the last was the delight in destruction. Mike's appeal in battle became quickly obvious. It was the delight in destruction. With punches flying, feet kicking and heads butting, the clan soon endured enough punishment. Once again they began a hasty retreat. At the time, I saw no reason as victors to pursue a retreating enemy, but not Mike. For him, their retreat had triggered an impulse to pursue and destroy. As the enemy escaped down the alley, Mike led the charge with the rest of us right behind him.

When the clan raced into their backyard, they quickly split into two groups. Several took refuge in the home, and the remaining sought sanctuary within the wooden outhouse. With all clan members either locked in the house or barricaded in the outhouse, I concluded we had dealt the enemy a terrible defeat, not to mention a devastating blow to their egos. Forcing the clan to cower for a second time in their yard was a glorious repeat of the first encounter. But victory was made even sweeter by the fact that we had accomplished the feat with fewer warriors than our first engagement. In addition, the humiliation of those hiding in a stinky two-hole latrine was frosting on the cake.

For Mike, the experience was more exhilarating. By Glenn's own definition, Mike had become overwhelmed by the delight of his enemy's destruction. In fact, his delight was so excessive he could not cease his hostility. Thus began the brutal battle for possession of the outhouse.

Frantically Mike began prying and beating with his fists to gain access. When every attempt failed, he endeavored to push the outhouse over on its side. However, due to the size of the structure and the weight of its occupants, he failed again.

Instead of relenting in his efforts to gain entry, Mike became even more emotionally resolved to succeed. By now, the outhouse had been under siege for more than fifteen minutes. Returning once more to the latch on the door he began kicking like a mule. Hovering above the entrance was a round moon shaped opening. It provided the only source of light and probably much needed ventilation.

Unbeknown to Mike, those being held captive were not totally without means. While Mike tugged on the door latch, someone inside slipped a large rock through the hole. The rock slammed squarely down on its intended target, Mike's head. The blow caused him to stumble forward until he came to rest against the outhouse.

For a moment, Mike appeared shaken. Everything was strangely quiet, like right before a hurricane strikes or a volcano erupts. I could not help but think that whoever pelted Mike with the rock had made a most terrible mistake. As we continued to wait for the drama to unfold, Mike's rage suddenly erupted. He grabbed the one thing that had prevented his earlier attempts to enter the outhouse and proceeded to bash the door using the rock as a battering ram.

When the wooden entry splintered and finally crumbled, Mike single-handedly jumped inside with fists clenched. He attacked the enemy in a fierce hand-to-hand combat. The fury of his savage spirit resounded in the cries of anguish echoing within the confines of the wooded structure. Bodies could be heard slamming against the walls. One by one, a bruised enemy retreated from the outhouse and scrambled to take refuge within the house. Like some barroom brawl, no one escaped without some torn clothing and a few memorable bruises.

When our tattered combatant finally emerged from the outhouse shaking and trembling, it was apparent that nothing was going to quell his anger. Without any hesitation, he prepared to storm the entire house. All sense of reason had taken flight. He was like a wild predator in pursuit of the fresh blood trail of a wounded prey. Fearful of what could happen if Mike's rage carried over to the house, we began to think quickly and talk even faster.

First, we cautioned Mike that their father had a shotgun. If he attempted to enter the house, one of the boys might use the gun. More important, neighbors might have already called the constable. They had done it before in our last provocation in this very house. I knew if Mike feared anyone, it would be the constable, for he already had more than his share of entanglements with the law.

Crowding around our newly found hero to prevent an assault on the house, we began cheering and boasting of his undaunted bravery and fierce courage. We also reminded him that his papers had not yet been delivered. However, we were more that happy to assist him in making his deliveries. No one wanted his customers to become angry for not receiving their paper on time. After several desperate minutes of constant persuasion, tranquility slowly replaced Mike's uncontrollable rage. We then took him by the arm and commenced a second victory march to commemorate our conquest.

This time the victory parade was for a different reason. We were marching to a different beat. We had challenged the enemy face to face in open combat on the battlefield in defense of our territory and walked away triumphant. There was no doubt that the hero of the day was Mike. In our minds, he had drawn a clear image of true courage as to how an individual could be a majority of one.

However, unleashing the unpredictable rage of an uncontrollable weapon proved to be scarier than the enemy. In later years, I learned that Mike had been sent to prison. For Mike, the path from hero to villain may have always been only a breath away. But the memory of his lion-hearted bravery and Herculean strength has remained forever.

Not every encounter with the clan erupted into a major battle. In many instances, both sides would randomly happen upon one or the other. Sometimes a confrontation ensued, and at other times, nothing happened. But more often then not, confrontation seemed inevitable during that summer of hostilities.

I recall an early evening when I strolled down a graveled alley to raid a favorite apple tree. Dr. Kincade's backyard had several good trees. Unlike John Henry he had a more generous heart and was a great doctor. Unexpectedly, three members of the clan discovered themselves traveling down the same route. No doubt, it was for the same reason.

As soon as they sighted my presence, they glanced at each other. I immediately sensed there was going to be a problem. Preparing to engage the enemy, I reached for my slingshot in one pocket, and a rock in the other. With the graceful flight of a deer and the endurance of a mule, they had little chance to catch me. But like a pack of hungry hounds eager for the chase, I knew they would give it a good try. Quickening the pace, I slipped a rock into my sling. Outnumbered three to one, the elimination of at least one pursuer seemed like a reasonable plan.

Rounding the block, I carefully calculated the distance between them and my slingshot. As I slowed down, I turned and fired a missile. The rock found its intended target, striking the arm of the lead runner. Unfortunately, the blow had not achieved its objective. Without skipping a beat, my hand reached deep into my pocket for a second rock. When the timing was again right, I turned and fired a second volley.

This time, one of the pursuers crashed to the ground. At first, the other two continued their pursuit, but even with an angry zeal they failed to close the distance. Finally, they with-drew and returned to the side of their fallen brother. The ordeal seemed like a crowning moment for a young warrior. I had faced a superior number and achieved a silent moment of triumph.

A week later, a similar incident occurred. Typically, on Friday night young people packed the Orpheum Theatre on Main Street. With a nickel and a dime in my pocket, I could purchase a ticket for ten cents and a bag of popcorn for five cents. Soda pop was never permitted in the theatre unless one sneaked it in.

Movies that played on Friday and Saturday featured gun-smoking westerns, bloody war battles, gangsters, or a jungle adventure like *Tarzan*. On Sunday and Monday, movies were a boring combination of music, dancing, and romancing. Fred Astair, Ginger Rogers, and Gene Kelly were much more suitable for adults; they were too boring for us young adventurers.

On this particular evening, the journey from the theater to home began as a leisurely stroll on the sidewalk. For most individuals that would seem normal, but for me it was a rare event. Typically when the sun went down, I meandered back and forth through numerous backyards under the cover of dark. The shadowed landmarks that had been imprinted into my memory by day made me invisible at night.

Traveling behind bushes and through neighborhood gardens in the shadows was not only safer, but an adventure unto itself. In the early 1950s, it was popular for people to spend evenings relaxing on the porch as they conversed in the summer breeze. The advantage of being able to blend into the background was that one could secretly listen to conversations everywhere. It must have been a trait I picked up from Grannie and her porch.

Those who reveled in idle chatter were never short on subjects. There was the rumor about an elderly rich man who slept on a couch in meager surroundings. That turned out to be quite accurate. John Wimmer had no formal education, yet, he would, in years to come, donate in excess of $600,000 to help with the medical clinic, nursing home, churches, and a number of small homes for seniors throughout the county. In present-day dollars, his contributions would have amounted to somewhere between four and five million dollars.

Then there was talk about the unredeemable who had violated the eleventh Commandment that stated, "A Catholic shall not marry or date a Protestant" and visa versa.

Even the Latin teacher was high on their list for more reasons than one. Of course, rumors about bankers were always popular. I should have taken warning before giving up the practice of law to become a banker. They were split on the local banker, who apparently married a woman half his age. Most women thought it was deplorable. However, men were careful not to openly disagree in the presence of their wives, but secretly they envied the old boy. The other banker was apparently no saint either. His big mansion next to the hospital was shrouded in a number of scandals that were almost unmentionable.

But my interest was never in the gossip or rumors. It was only in the challenge of seeing without being seen. About halfway home, I had decided to move from the sidewalk to the middle of the street. While Main Street had sufficient lighting, the residential area, in contrast, had very little illumination. With a state of war in effect, any dimly lighted sidewalk in the evening compromised safety by providing an opportunity for an ambush. And there was no doubt that adversaries were looking for some serious payback.

In our small community, residential blocks were lighted by one single lamp at the end of each block. It offered no brighter illumination than an ordinary household light bulb. The bright fluorescent streetlights of today had not come of age. Actually, if my eyes were acclimated to the dark, I achieved better visibility without the light on the pole.

Approaching the intersection three blocks from home, I noticed that two medium-sized silhouettes had entered the street like a pair of gunfighters from Dodge City or Tombstone. As I strained to get a glimpse of whether these mysterious figures were friend or foe, the appearance of their stalking body language suggested they were not friendly. I had learned from experience to be wary of shadows, especially those that moved.

When both silhouettes bolted in my direction, I dashed off like a squirrel jumped by a fox. With a combination of speed and knowledge of the turf in the dark, I was equipped with a pair of good equalizers. My first decision was to make a trial run to determine how serious these pursuers were in catching their prey. After a block of serious running, it was clear they were committed to the race.

Success in winning a foot race was not dependent on speed alone, but in how efficiently one could control breathing. Forced to succumb to a lack of oxygen, muscles soon became fatigued, and the race was lost. For some, the uncanny ability to control breathing came naturally, but more often it took a lot of practice.

One girl in our grade had acquired that magic. She was country born. Racing with the wind across the open prairie, she had evolved into a natural, swift runner. Whenever we played a running game like Capture the Flag, or Pump, Pump Pull Away at youth gatherings in church, Eileen moved with the inherent grace of an antelope. With both her speed and looks, this future Homecoming Queen was always quite a catch. However, very few ever succeeded.

In contrast, I had managed to perfect my own technique by racing along the highway ditches in search of empty pop bottles and charging back and forth from the river. The result of such exercise was a most effective weapon—endurance. On a long distance foot race, endurance made the difference between escape and being captured. A preacher man had already taught me that lesson.

Into the third block, I recognized the two silhouettes as older brothers of the enemy clan. Now I had a serious crisis. It was time to consummate one of those contingency plans for escape specifically reserved for such an occasion.

Racing across several backyards and then dipping into an alley, my path was leading directly to the home of an elderly grandmother who had a very large porch on the front of her house. Planted around the deck were bushes as thick as cattails in a swamp. As for the porch itself, it was boarded to the ground on all sides. However, in the far corner next to the house was a loose board. If properly turned, it would create an opening large enough to allow a small frame to squeeze through. Once underneath, the loose board could be returned to cover the trail.

I had practiced this maneuver often for just this kind of an emergency. The actual escape required only a few seconds. Therefore, my pursuers had to be just the right distance behind to allow enough time to disappear from their view. Once beneath the porch, I would be committed like a rabbit to his burrow. But unlike the rabbit's hole in the ground, this burrow was stocked with a supply of rocks, a spear and a club. And this rabbit knew how to use those weapons. Anyone dumb enough to crawl under a dark, narrow, and unknown porch would soon learn a painful lesson in carefully selecting a battleground.

If everything else failed, the alternative plan was to beat on the house from beneath the porch. The noise would arouse the attention of Grandma. She would most likely turn on the outside lights. Upon seeing intruders, she would yell and threaten to call the constable. We certainly know by now this would be taken as a serious threat. No one in his right mind ever wanted to be confronted by the local constable. Furthermore, neighbors would also hear the commotion and quickly rush to Grandma's assistance. In either scenario, the pursuers would flee without any hesitation.

Making the final dash from the alley, my legs picked up the pace as I scurried around the house and dove for the porch. In seconds, I was safely tucked away out of sight. Lying perfectly quiet except for a heart hammering to the beat of a drum, I listened for the sound of feet stomping the ground. In moments of suspense like this, a person unconsciously holds his breath as the body tenses for that final moment of judgment.

I soon recognized the pounding of footsteps approaching. When one of the clan shouted, "He must have gone that way," I breathed a sigh of relief. Waiting ten minutes in complete, reverent silence was the final chapter to another skillful, but close escape.

Neither victory nor escape was ever a given. Sometimes we used to play at the school grounds. We especially enjoyed sliding down the metal cylinder that functioned as an emergency escape in case of fire. On this particular day, one of the clan silently crept up from behind and knocked me face down to the ground. As I rolled to my back, he bounced squarely on the top of my chest. Pinned by someone twice my size, I was hopelessly trapped. When two friends came to my assistance, the attacker clenched a threatening fist. He then turned and snarled, "If anyone dares to come any closer, I will bash his face!"

In response to his threat, they halted and waited for me to make the final call. Judging from the fearless expression on the Grim Reaper's face, I was definitely a goner. Squeezing both eyes shut to await the inevitable, I yelled, "To hell with him. Get 'im off me!"

No sooner were such brave words spoken, a fierce blow like a kick of a mule was delivered to the left side of my nose. The second blow smacked the other side of my face with the force of a Joe Louis punch, causing every nerve connection immediately to shut down. It was like being suddenly submerged in frigid ice water. The shock mentally numbed my entire sensory board. I do not remember anything after that last blow.

Fifty years later, the restriction of air passing through my left nostril remains an annoying remembrance of that incident. I never again made the same mistake in confusing bravery with stupidity. At the time, I accepted the broken nose as a badge of honor without the Purple Heart. But it also served as a painful reminder of the bitter taste of defeat.

History has dictated that, in every war, one battle or major event often turns the tide of the conflict and brings closure. In the Napoleonic War, it was Waterloo. In the Civil War, it was Gettysburg. For Japan in World War II, it was Hiroshima.

It was near the end of summer in our war with the clan. A resolution remained nowhere in sight. The fantasy had begun to fade. It was replaced with thoughts of returning to the classroom. We fully understood that this war could not be brought to the playground or the school hallways. The school principal had the ability to become both a Hitler and SS Storm Trooper with the authority and force to vanquish both sides at his whim.

With the window of opportunity to finish the war about to close, the decision was made to marshal all the forces for a final showdown. In the fort near the fairgrounds, we planned what would be our version of D-Day on the shores of the muddy river. Our objective was to attack with everything we had and reclaim our rafts, confiscated a week earlier.

The battle plan was simple. We would split our forces in half and surround the opposition. The strategy was to attack from opposite directions simultaneously. Sam would lead one group. The remainder would attack under my command. When our force reached the rendezvous point near the rafts, we would signal the attack with a raised t-shirt banner.

Reconnaissance had reported that the clans were currently on the river playing on our rafts. Once we surrounded the enemy and established a posture that provided no escape, the plan was to pulverize the enemy into surrendering with a barrage of rocks powered by hand and slingshot.

Crucial to the success of our mission was reaching the designated positions without being discovered. Sam and his group intended to head away from the river, and then double back through the alley leading to the river. This would give us more time to go the longer distance. From the alley they would crawl undetected to a broken down-structure located above the rafts. There, they would lay in wait for the rest of us to make the circle and attack from along the river. Under no circumstances were they to engage the enemy until our forces initiated the attack.

As the troops moved out, not a word was spoken. Everyone understood this was going to be the battle for all the marbles. What we did not know was how many of the enemy would be entrenched at the river. It was always a dangerous gamble to divide a fighting force. Especially if one is uncertain as to the deployment of the enemy. But as in every successful venture, the degree of risk was often the price one paid to gain an advantage. Besides, Mike had shown us that winning was not always measured in mere numbers. The heart of even one individual full of righteous fury was enough to become an invincible force.

Carefully maneuvering from home to home to avoid detection, every combatant was committed and prepared to close the final chapter in our fight for freedom. Reaching the last structure on the block, we huddled in a circle to make sure that everyone understood the plan. Minutes later, the point man scouting the terrain ahead flashed the all-clear signal.

Leapfrogging into the grassy field leading to the river, we vanished amid the dense foliage. Any chance for the enemy to spot our advance was now slim to none. Hugging the river's edge, neither the thick patches of burning grass nor the sharp, pointed stickers could dampen our determination. As we crept closer to the intended rendezvous point, a deadly stillness hung in the air. The only sound was the solo rapture of a red-winged blackbird perched on a cattail along the shoreline.

Crouched low to the ground, we were prepared to launch the surprise attack. The T-shirt banner was raised to signal the others to attack. Breaking the silence, we sprang from the tall grass yelling our battle cry. But to everyone's surprise, there was no response. The enemy was not in sight. We were at a loss. We knew they had been close to the rafts only an hour earlier. Where could they be?

My immediate thought was that maybe the enemy was waiting in hiding to spring their own surprise. The thick vegetation provided ample opportunity for them to hide. At that moment, anything seemed possible. Finally, I shouted out the order to make a run for the rafts. If we were to be attacked, our chances were better to make a fight with our backs to the river. With eyes fixated on the rafts, we raced towards the water. Nothing happened.

With neither Sam nor the enemy anywhere in sight, we decided to venture further up river. Along the trail, the only evidence of human intrusion was the presence of several crunched candy wrappings. A few minutes later, in a clearing surrounded by large cottonwood trees, we discovered Sam's body lying slumped at the base of a cottonwood.

At first, I thought my eyes were deceived by some nightmarish illusion. At our feet was the unconscious body of Sam with arms outstretched around the trunk of a tree. Both wrists were tightly bound by twine. Crumpled near his side lay the remnants of a T-shirt saturated in blood.

Being tightly lashed to the tree had prevented the body from dropping completely to the ground. His head lay perfectly still as though nothing seemed to disturb the profound silence of a boy gone to sleep. I remembered staring but not believing. In fact, the entire scene was reminiscent of the picture of Rip Van Winkle on the cover of my storybook. Both Rip and Sam appeared to be in the same deep sleep. Their motionless bodies had come to be at peace with the world.

Washington Irving captured the moment when he wrote:

> *They suddenly stared at him with*
> *such fixed statute-like gaze. . . .*
> *that his heart turned within him*
> *and his knees smote together.*
> *At length his senses were overpowered,*
> *his eyes swam in his head and*
> *the head gradually declined, and*
> *he fell into a deep sleep.*

As we cautiously approached, one could not help but notice the deep, jagged lines cut into the flesh of Sam's back. Some lines were a series of red, blistering welts while others had raw flesh laid bare with blood oozing from the wound.

Until that very moment, no one had ever given serious consideration to the real perils of warfare. We never expected to achieve success without a few casualties, but not like this. Out of nowhere, the real face of war had unexpectedly jumped out and smacked us with a sharp blow. When it did, we lost focus on the reasons we ever went to war in the first place. More important, that misguided feeling of invincibility was forever shattered.

From the very beginning, our war was to be glorious, daring and a challenge of wits. The prospect of being seriously wounded or taken prisoner and mutilated was never a part of the masquerade. Bravery in the movies had always been portrayed as a glamorous virtue. Now it lay before us revealed as the brutal and unforgiving heresy it really was. With our innocence lost, we could only gaze at a hideous, crumbled body awash in blood while our minds remained frozen in disbelief. The sense of glory in the ideal warrior had been destroyed.

Once the initial shock passed, we instinctively scrambled to assist Sam in any way possible. I severed the cord of twine while others held Sam to prevent him from falling on his wounds. Using the signal shirt as a sponge, we gathered water from the river to wash and clean the crusted dry blood around his wounds. The touch of cold water stimulated Sam's body to quiver. Unexpectedly, he blinked back to consciousness.

A great wave of relief spread through us when we realized Sam's injuries appeared far worse than they were. Immediately more questions were asked than he could answer. After a long sip of water from a canteen, he began to relate the story of his ordeal. Apparently the enemy had somehow become aware that his force was moving towards the river. With that crucial knowledge in hand, they devised their own plan of encirclement and destruction.

Once Sam realized they were trapped, he decided to decoy the enemy to allow his comrades to escape. As for Sam, he would take a different course of action, one that took a lot of courage. Abandoning any idea to cut and run he launched his own offensive. With an indomitable fighting spirit he had acquired from his experience with Mike, he single-handedly attacked the younger members of the clan.

He anticipated that his assault on the youngest would draw the older siblings to their rescue. In that unwavering sacrifice, he provided precious time for his own younger combatants to escape. As I listened to his story, there was no doubt in my mind that Sam had firmly resolved to perish gloriously. His description sounded like a script out of the movies.

He went on to share that he expected to pay a measurable price for pounding on the younger members of the clan. Incensed by his attack, they accused him of being a "dirty coward" because he had picked on the youngest and weakest. And in the heat of their anger, they bound him to the tree. Then the younger brothers acted out their own form of retaliation with whips.

As they flogged away, he remembered that the blows came so quickly it felt and sounded like machine gun fire ripping into his flesh. Overcome by a combination of pain and heat, he finally retreated by closing his eyes and curling into the tree. He could not remember passing out.

We surmised that when he slipped into unconsciousness, the clan became frightened. For all they knew, their captive could have been beaten into a mindless state. And the very possibility of having caused another human to go straight from life to nonexistence must have been terrifying to them. When Sam finished, I pondered if I could have done the same. Apparently courage can cause people to do remarkable things. But if they knew the outcome, would their choice be the same?

The choices we were now confronted with created their own terrible dilemma. Sam appeared to need more medical attention than we could provide by the river. But if we took him to the doctor, someone would inevitably call the constable. That would result in even more serious consequences.

Our second thought was to bring Sam home. However, in his present bloody condition his mother would flip out. The wrath of parental anger could lead to a number of unthinkable consequences. Up to this point, parents still had no idea of our on-going mischievous activities.

Finally, we decided the safer alternative was for Sam to remain overnight at my home. He would call his mother at work to let her know he would be eating and camping out in our back-yard. Since it was summer, the idea would not arouse suspicion. As for my mother, she never returned from work at the beauty shop before 5:30. Already accustom to my camping out in the evenings, she would not have any reason to be suspicious.

The plan would provide an entire afternoon for us to tend to his wounds. And considering the angry red streaks on his back, that extra time was crucial. In addition, Sam not only had the rest of the day to recuperate, he had the night and the entire next day to heal. We hoped by the day after, he would be far enough along to fake his condition to his mother.

Fathers in those days were seldom a problem concerning a child's daily state of health. They normally worked late and were too tired to give much notice to children. But mothers were a different story. They were religiously attentive and especially keen on their children's health.

Fortunately, mothers took precautions to give sons wider latitude in privacy concerning their physical body. The explanation more than likely had to do with the same reason mothers never coached their sons on the subject of sex. Whether they themselves were embarrassed or thought we might be embarrassed, their discreet behavior now worked to our advantage.

In the ensuing week, we waited anxiously to hear if any-one in the neighborhood caught wind of the incident. As the days passed, everything continued to remain calm. Even the clan was noticeably absent. No doubt they were harboring their own uncertainties, not the least of which was retaliation. If so, they would have been justifiably correct.

During those anxious days of recovery, the utmost thought on our minds was to plan an appropriate response. Like a brewing thunderstorm on the open prairie gathering intensity, we were preparing to unleash our own brand of fury. The enemy's transgressions had gone far beyond the prescribed rules of fair play. And although no Code of Behavior for engagement had ever been agreed upon, we assumed that everyone understood that there would be boundaries of decency that both sides would not cross. Mutilation was an obvious indiscretion.

We were faced with two options. We could either capitulate or make an appropriate response. Unanimously we concluded that if the whipping was a forecast of what was yet to come, the clan had to be held accountable. They had to be forced to understand that when the terms of fair play are violated, they themselves might suffer similar or even worse consequences.

With that decision in hand, our minds began to navigate between what would be deemed justifiable retaliation and what was reasonably necessary to get the message across. Unknown to most Americans, including ourselves, U.S. soldiers had experienced extreme, agonizing brutality at the hands of the Japanese. As combatants, they would mutilate and execute their prisoners in the most primitive and barbaric fashion. As a result, many concluded that the Japanese had no sense of morality. In response, some Americans acted out their own forms of cruelty. Torturous and brutal deaths were sanctified in the name of retaliation.

By all accounts, these acts of transgression transformed the warrior from within. He unconsciously capitulated to the dark side with a cold and callous heart. The resulting consequence escalated the cruelty until a state of barbarous hostility existed between both warring factions. By war's end, a deep, hidden evil had taken control and brought out the very worst in human nature.

That same senseless pattern of escalation was about to happen in our war. We too were blindly determined to make the enemy think differently about future acts of brutality. We had no way to know that any savage reaction might only worsen the situation. In fact, it could set into motion a dangerous and vicious cycle of more cruelty.

Oblivious to our own reality, we had become guided more by thoughts of vengeance than a benign willingness to forgive. If God had been expected to play a part in our war, this would have been a good time for him to make an appearance.

Fortunately, the tactic we decided upon was a sinister plan designed more to intimidate than do bodily harm. The following week we executed a trap that captured one of the younger clan members who had whipped Sam. Marching the young prisoner to the river where the whipping took place, we symbolically bound his hands with the same twine used on Sam. But instead of using a tree, we opted to place our quarry on a raft. Once securely situated near the center, the captive watched in terror as we doused the outer edges of the raft with gasoline.

Before we ignited the gas into flames and shoved the raft into the flow of the river, we informed the prisoner that we had a message for him to deliver. If they were to ever repeat another act of brutality as was done to Sam, what we were about to do here would be only a small dose of the real wrath they could expect.

As we readied to strike the match, the captive remained tightly huddled as he trembled in fear of the prospect of being set afloat on a blazing raft. He thought he was facing two dreadful expectations. One, he might end up joining the fish on the bottom, or he could become morning toast. In reality, we knew neither of those outcomes could ever happen.

First, the splashing of water would quickly douse the flame. Second, water-logged wood does not burn. Third, the water level was shallow enough to wade to shore whenever he collected enough courage to make his jump for freedom. As a final precaution, we remained hidden in the bushes nearby to make certain his escape was safely carried out.

In the movies, revenge had always been portrayed as sweet. Our experience was anything but sweet. The pitiful sight and sound of our young captive crying created a sickening feeling in everyone. And despite all the precautions we had taken, we consciously began to regret ever considering such a dastardly deed. But all we could do was take comfort in the rationalization that in war some miseries were just unavoidable. That was not an original concept either. It was part of a movie script. Sometimes it was expressed as "War is hell."

Whatever message was ultimately delivered home, or how our threat had been perceived, the river incident became the final encounter of the war. A non-negotiated peace prevailed without ceremony. I like to believe that both sides had come to a realization that it was time for an unspoken truce. The character of war had changed dramatically. Each side had crossed over the line. I am certain no one ever wanted a serious incident that we would regret for the rest of our lives.

The war unofficially ended with a cessation of hostilities. There was no animosity in our hearts toward any of the participants. No one harbored any malice or thoughts of revenge. Both sides were willing to look beyond the past with a willingness to settle our differences as we aspired to bring a sense of harmony back into our lives. The truce also brought the period of the little boy warrior to an abrupt end.

After all these years, it still remains difficult to understand why we considered fighting such a noble concept. Maybe it was predictable. Could it be that most males inherit an instinctive measure of aggression that has to be reckoned with? And if it was an unconscious inborn trait, has it always been accepted as natural behavior?

Unquestionably, the stirring images of battle in the war movies and its pictorialization in the ten-cent war comics absorbed our innocent and untested minds. Together, they created an environment that set us upon a course of reckless behavior to seek out the glory of battle. Napoleon said: "Death is nothing; but to live defeated and without glory is to die every day."

When the smoke had cleared from our battlefields, I came away with a different understanding of war. It was no longer defined in terms of glory or exciting adventures, but rather as an explicit reminder of how savage and cruel humans can become when fueled by the sights and non-pleasantries of combat.

Despite uncovering the darker side of human nature, the other experiences of my warrior period proved to be a valuable learning episode. Face-to-face confrontation with both the simple and complicated problems had provided a testing ground to examine individual strengths and weaknesses. It nurtured a new and unknown courage never to fear to stand alone with my convictions.

Filled with a new sense of confidence, a new world had opened at a most appropriate time. I was about to begin the ritual passage from grade school to junior high. Mike had demonstrated that without the right kind of courage, a person was always vulnerable to fear and failure. I would never again sell myself short in achieving any goal that I really wanted. Maybe Mike had also discovered a new world by his own courage. After prison, I heard he eventually moved to California and became an artist.

No one escaped the strong influence that World War II had on everyone in our generation, especially the very young.

Even though we were far from the actual war, the movies, comics, and radio had created a strong mental link between that conflict and our own behavior. The media outreach had successfully established a variety of powerful war stereotypes for us to mimic.

We were the children of war. We marched to the tune of the time by improvising toy weapons to hunt down every "Jap" and "Nazi" hiding in every bush or grove of trees in America. We tossed stones as grenades, and regrettably, we were even willing to make war on each other.

World War II was a necessary war that had to be fought and won. I would never reach the same conclusion about our war. We had no winners, only losers in the knowledge of what could have happened. In hindsight, just maybe some spiritual deity had found its own way to participate in the war.

---

# CONCLUSION

O UR MEMORY IS the key that will unlock the past. To capture a memory is like discovering a butterfly for the first time. Both are inherently beautiful to behold and even more wonderful to share. As we grow older, we naturally tend to relive the memorable moments of earlier times. We begin to reconnect with our childhood settings. For some, there is an unexplainable urge to revisit the sounds, sights, and smells of those days long gone by.

Those who choose to follow their instincts and return to their roots will find mixed emotions. The reality of recapturing the memory may prove to be as difficult as losing it. People and places have vanished forever. Gone for me were the aromas of freshly baked bread and pastries, like scrumptious white-frosted Bismarck's with red jelly or the crushed peanut-covered mocha bars from Parson's Bakery.

Gone too were the old, wooden barrels filled with fresh, dilled pickles floating in a brine mixture strong enough to clear a plugged nose, surrounded by stacks of dry goods in C.R. Andrews & Company. I also missed the tinkling of the bell

215

signaling the metal cup moving up the cable at J.C. Penny Co. And I especially missed the loud music of the jukebox playing my favorite rock song in Slatt's Malt Shop while sipping a cherry coke.

But most disturbing was the discovery that each has vanished without any trace of ever existing. Unexpectedly, I slowly began to realize the birthplace of beginning actually loses the memory of our own existence. However, do not become disheartened, for change has always been inevitable.

Parents, grandparents, and countless other generations have experienced the same evolution in their own lifetime. I remember as a child listening to grown-ups commenting more than once on how "life was no longer like the good old days." At the time, I never understood why they were so preoccupied in reliving the past. Only now do I appreciate the emotional satisfaction they must have shared in seeking comfort in a personal memory from days gone by. For them, the yesteryears were not as inaccessible as we might think. Like an old scar, they had never left in the first place.

As our lives evolve to maturity, the child within still hibernates in our subconscious mind. It is patiently waiting to be rediscovered. I urge everyone who reads this legacy to take whatever time is required to reacquaint themselves with his or her own past. And when one begins to reconnect with the child hidden deep within the forgotten dust of memory, find comfort in knowing that these memories are a timeless treasure worth sharing.

If we bind these memories in the hearts of those we love and leave behind, a valuable part of us will never die. And generations now and those yet to come will learn and benefit from the many experiences encountered on our journey through life. We must accept that we have a moral responsibility to leave them more than just a grave stone with a name and a date.

We need to recognize that life itself cannot be measured by time alone without consideration of how far we have traveled. The memories we carry are like the air we breathe. When they are gone, there is nothing left.

By merging the past with the present, the writing of this book became a reflection of my entire existence. And while most things are forgotten, the memoirs we reduce to writing are preserved for all times. It is my hope that this book will endure as a valuable, living testament to generations I will never come to know as it reveals the adventures and lessons learned by *The Boy My Children Never Knew*.

# EPILOGUE

A T SOME POINT in our journey, we begin to ponder how good life has been to us. Searching for a report card, we seek answers to questions. Did we live the best life possible? Were the struggles and sacrifices worth the rewards? Did we make a small difference somewhere or in someone? Can the memory be preserved when we die?

As we progress through life, we slowly appreciate the wisdom that comes with the years. We realize that wisdom may not have come at all, so we do not reject it just because it comes late. Fifty years would pass before I realized that the boy I was and the man I would come to be were one in the same. These two lives had secretly intertwined like the waters of a river. Ever growing together, their life force eventually wove a fabric of coexistence that would bind the past with the future.

In every living human being, we are able to discover something that identifies who we are. At birth, each of us inherits a unique genetic blueprint with personalized traits that no one can take away. As parents and grandparents fade away, so do our opportunities to discover those unique characteristics that they brought to life. That loss is everyone's loss.

Native Americans understood that "only the rocks will live forever." The same can be said of life. Like time, it flows by as a relentless river with no return. No sooner does one life come into being, it hurries past for another to be born and swept away in its own time.

However, if we salvage life's experiences from that river of time, we can bind our beginning to the end. Together, they will emerge as canons of knowledge that will leave a road map for others to consider on their own journey through life.

# ABOUT THE AUTHOR

ORN IN THE HEART of the Red River Valley in West Central Minnesota near the Dakota border, the author captures the adventures and memories of early childhood. Kidnapped by a child predator from the carnival at the age of six and placed under the sentence of death, the author shares this experience as only a survivor can tell it.

Never forgetting the past, he brings the reader on a journey that embraces the passion and unrelenting energy of a child's search for adventure. It is a journey of both simplistic and sometimes death-defying proportions. The book is dedicated to the principle that within every individual we are able to discover something that identitfies who we are. It is a unique genetic blueprint with personalized traits that no one can take away, and valuable testament to pass on to future generations.

In his spare time, Rodger nurtures the forest and wildlife on the land where he and his wife, Lynn, established a family business known as Little Elk Ranch. Started in the 1970s, the horse camp for children continues. In addition, he is the CEO and attorney to one of the larger family-owned and operated banks in Minnesota. He has dedicated a career to preserve the history and the financial growth of a banking heritage that dates back to 1881. Often referred to as the "Log Bank," it is properly known as American Heritage National Bank with locations in St. Cloud, Long Prairie, and Browerville, Minnesota.